The
TAPIR
SCIENTIST

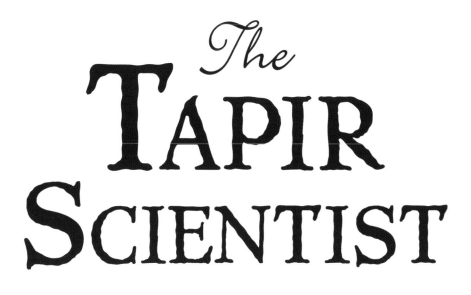

The
TAPIR
SCIENTIST

Text by *Sy Montgomery*

Photographs by *Nic Bishop*

Houghton Mifflin Books for Children • Houghton Mifflin Harcourt • Boston New York 2013

For Gabriel and Duda:
Wishing you a lifetime of loving and protecting nature

Text copyright © 2013 by Sy Montgomery
Photographs copyright © 2013 by Nic Bishop

Photo credit page(s):
2, 39, 53, 54, 71, 75, 77, back flap (right): Pati Medici
38: Karen Taylor
23, 24, 70: Dorothée Ordonneau
64: Arnaud Desbiez

Houghton Mifflin Books for Children is an imprint of Houghton Mifflin Harcourt Publishing Company.

www.hmhbooks.com

The text of this book is set in Adobe Jenson Pro.
Maps and tapir paintings by Cara Llewellyn

Library of Congress Cataloging-in-Publication Data
Montgomery, Sy.
The tapir scientist / written by Sy Montgomery ; photographed by Nic Bishop.
p. cm.
ISBN 978-0-547-81548-0
1. Tapirs—Brazil—Juvenile literature. 2. Tapirs—Research—Brazil—Juvenile literature.
3. Medici, Patricia, 1972– —Juvenile literature. I. Bishop, Nic, 1955– ill. II. Title.
QL737.U64M66 2013
599.66—dc23
2012018678

Manufactured in China
SCP 10 9 8 7 6 5 4 3 2 1
4500400570

Contents

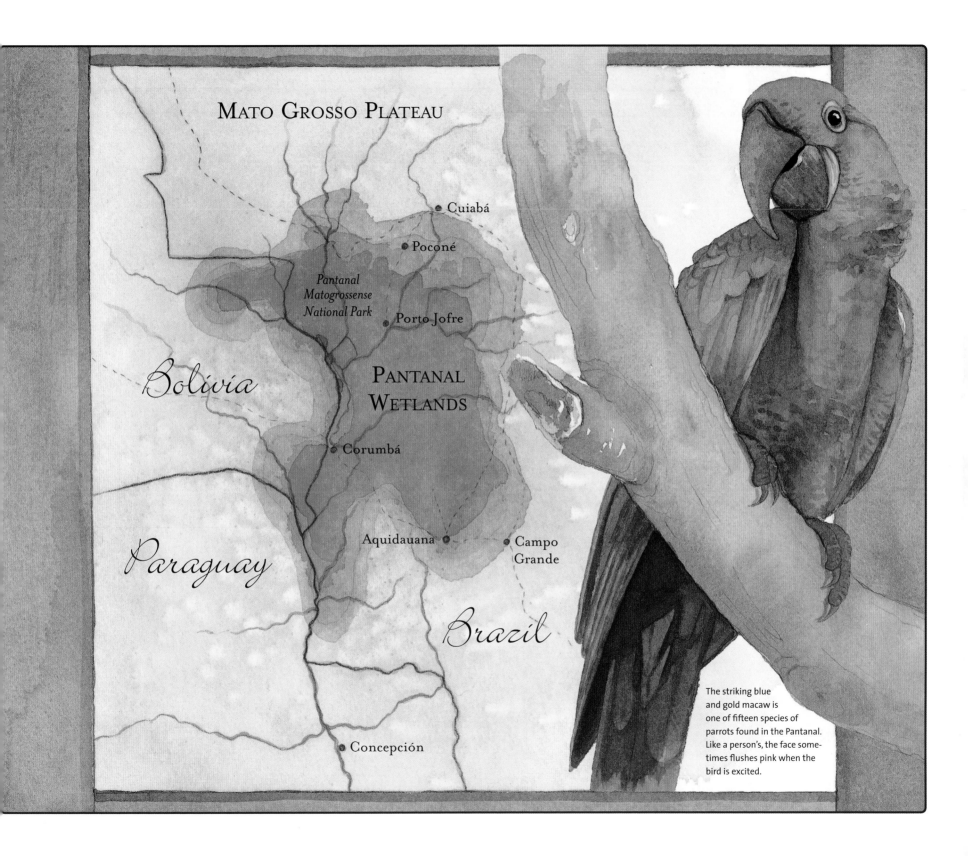

MATO GROSSO PLATEAU

Cuiabá

Poconé

Pantanal Matogrossense National Park

Porto Jofre

Bolivia

PANTANAL WETLANDS

Corumbá

Paraguay

Aquidauana

Campo Grande

Brazil

Concepción

The striking blue and gold macaw is one of fifteen species of parrots found in the Pantanal. Like a person's, the face sometimes flushes pink when the bird is excited.

Pati scans the Pantanal landscape for wildlife. This vast wetland is home to hundreds of species.

CHAPTER I

On the Tapir Trail

RAP-RAP-RAP!

José's knuckles bang the roof of the car. It's the sound we've been waiting for.

Crammed into the 1977 Toyota Bandeirante Land Cruiser, we've been scanning the grass, water, and scrubby forest around us for a big, dark shape. We're in the Pantanal—the world's largest wetland, ten times the size of the Everglades, a place shimmering with a million shades of green and pulsing with the songs and wing beats of birds. Standing in the open back of the vehicle, Pati's field assistant, José Maria de Aragão, has the best view—and now he's signaled us that he's spotted what we came from three continents to find: a tapir (TAY-peer). It's surely one of the weirdest-looking and most mysterious animals on earth.

Never heard of a tapir? You're not alone. Even here in Brazil, most citizens don't know what it is. In the United States, they don't either. When videographers visited a park in Orlando, Florida, to ask people what a tapir was, different folks told them it was a dangerous wild cat, a sort of monkey, and a huge bird. One person insisted it was green. Another said it lived in the tundra.

But the real tapir is more unexpected yet. A tropical animal with a long, flexible snout (which it can use as a snorkel when it swims) and a stout body, four hoofed toes on each front foot and three on each in back, it looks like a cross between a hippo, an elephant, and something prehistoric.

Tapirs aren't related to elephants or hippos. Because of their flexible snouts, some people think they're anteaters, but that's wrong, too; tapirs' closest relatives are rhinos and horses (they even whinny the way horses do!). But the tapir *is* prehistoric: it has remained unchanged since the Miocene, more than twelve million years ago—a time when mastodons, saber-toothed cats, and bear dogs roamed North America and the first humans had not yet evolved in Africa. A lot of other things have changed since then: A land bridge now connects North and South America. Horses back then had three toes on each foot; now each foot has but one. The mastodons, saber-tooths, and bear dogs are gone. But tapirs still look much the same.

Five million years ago, tapirs lived all over Europe, Asia, and the Americas. Now they're found only in South America, Central America, and Southeast Asia. The tapir is "a survivor of a more gentle and legendary time," as one long-ago traveler wrote, "wandering in unique isolation in a world not yet mature enough for its wisdom."

But Pati, a petite Brazilian with a huge smile and an iron will, is eager for tapir wisdom—for soon it might be too late. All four species of tapirs are disappearing, and what's even more terrible, whole forests could vanish with them.

Tapirs love fruit, and because they eat in one place and poop in another, they transport the seeds in the fruits they've eaten, taking them far from the trees on which they grew.

Pati calls the tapir "the gardener of the forest" because it "plants" (complete with fertilizer) the seeds that grow into trees upon whose fruit many other animals depend. Tapirs are too important to lose. Yet very little is known about them—including the best way to protect them.

Learning that is a job Pati takes personally. For her, conserving the forests and the animals is as important as protecting her own home.

Pati was born in São Paulo, the largest city in Brazil. When she was six, her mother and stepfather, who worked for Volkswagen in Brazil, moved to a house amid a mossy, humid forest between the outermost edge of the city and Brazil's Atlantic coast. There were few other houses and few other kids—but loads of trees, birds, and monkeys. "I never owned a doll," she explained. She never wanted one. "I just played in the forest. We kids would walk the trails in the forest, build huts in the forest. I loved that." In high school she thought she wanted to be an architect, but then she realized that she felt more at home in nature than in any building. She soon discovered that protecting the land and its animals was more important than any human-made structure she could design.

Pati started out studying monkeys. "But there were plenty of people concerned with primates," she said. "I wanted to start something new." In 1992 she

Pati has always loved the outdoors.

Pampas deer inhabit the drier grassland areas of the Pantanal. They are often preyed on by pumas.

Beautiful sunsets often adorn the Pantanal.

and nine others founded the Instituto de Pesquisas Ecológicas (Portuguese for Institute for Ecological Research). They made a list of "dream animals" that needed study. "The tapir was one of these," she said. "They're major seed dispersers, with a huge role in shaping and maintaining the forest. I wanted to know more. At that point we knew zero about tapirs in Brazil."

Why's that? "Because it's *so* difficult to study them," Pati explained. "They're hard to find. They're solitary. They are nocturnal [active mostly at night]. They're hard to capture. It's an animal that's extremely difficult to work with."

All of us have gathered on this latest expedition to study tapirs—and it will demand everything we've got. We'll follow them with the latest telemetry technology—and by looking for hoof prints in the sand. We'll search on foot, by car, and with motion-sensing camera traps. We'll need outdoor skills and language skills, knowledge of mechanics and medicine, and tools that range from sticks to satellites. Unraveling the secret lives of tapirs is at once like searching for clues in a detective story and watching a soap opera. As we're about to find out, it's a quest full of drama and challenge, mystery and danger.

For the next two weeks we'll be looking for the lowland tapir, the most widespread tapir of all. It's found in most of South America's grasslands and rainforests. (The Baird's tapir lives in Central and northern South America; the rare mountain tapir in South America in Colombia, Ecuador, and Peru; and the Malayan tapir, dark gray except for a broad white stripe around its middle, in Southeast Asia.) Maybe even this afternoon or this evening, we're hoping to dart one with a tranquilizer so

MALAYAN TAPIR

MOUNTAIN TAPIR

12

we can photograph, examine, and outfit it with a radio collar so Pati can track the animal's movements and find out, among other things, how much land each tapir needs to survive. It's a crucial first step to protecting this fascinating, widespread but little-known species. But first we have to find a tapir.

Just moments earlier Pati had told us to be ready in case we do. If José knocks, "no moving, no talking until we dart the tapir," she warned. Along with a sedative to make the animal sleep, she explained, the dart contains a radio transmitter that will allow the team to track it if it runs into the brush before it lies down to sleep. "We wait two to three minutes," Pati said. "We don't want to run after it or frighten or stress it—"

RAP-RAP-RAP!

At the sound of the knock Pati raises her binoculars. Is it really a tapir? A big, dark shape might be something else. It could be a giant anteater—a toothless beast with a tube-shaped head and huge bushy tail—which can stretch seven feet long. It could be one of the four species of deer here, grazing with its head down. It could be a long, low bush.

Or it could be a cow.

BAIRD'S TAPIR

LOWLAND TAPIR AND BABY

The tough zebu cattle raised by ranchers in the Pantanal originally came from India. They thrive despite hot summer temperatures.

A cow—wandering the wilds of Brazil?

You might not expect to find a cow in the Amazon rainforest. But you should here, in Brazil's other great, though lesser-known, wildlife area: the Pantanal (PAHN-tuh-NAHL). The name comes from the Portuguese word "to lick," for here the waters are always licking the land. Stretching for seventy-five thousand square miles during the wet season, the Pantanal is as big as the state of Florida, extending from southwestern Brazil into parts of Paraguay and Bolivia. It's a mixture of wet, subtropical forests and wet grasslands nourished by more than a hundred rivers. Described as "South America's Serengeti" and "the Everglades on steroids," it's packed with strange and beautiful animals. From the world's largest rodent, the capybara, to the world's largest parrot, the blue and gold macaw, to the world's largest gatherings of crocodiles, yacare caimans, the Pantanal swarms with superlatives.

But it's also full of cows and horses—with some pigs, sheep, and goats thrown in for good measure. Most of the Pantanal is not a national park or a nature reserve. Ninety-five percent of the area is privately owned by ranchers, whose eight million cattle share the land with the native animals. The spot we're in now is actually a huge paddock, one of twenty, on a sixty-five-square-mile ranch known as Baía das Pedras, whose owners welcome Pati's study of tapirs.

The capybara is a four-foot-long semiaquatic rodent. It feeds mostly on grasses and water plants.

Wild pigs in the Pantanal are descended from domestic animals that were released by early settlers.

Gabriel sits in the back of the Land Cruiser, ready with his dart gun.

Pati brings her binoculars down from her eyes. False alarm. "*Um porco*," she says in Portuguese, the national language of Brazil. A feral pig. A really big feral pig.

We drive on. Each of us is eager to get a chance to do what we've come here for: Pati, the leader of the expedition, hopes to dart, examine, and collar as many tapirs as possible. José has had much experience tracking tapirs with Pati through the bush for the past sixteen years. Gabriel Damasceno, with both Brazilian and American citizenship, is ready with his dart gun. Two veterinarians, Brazilian Eduardo Moreno and Dorothée Ordonneau, a volunteer from France, are here to see if the tapirs are healthy and to ensure that the darting goes safely. Photographer Nic Bishop

and I, Sy Montgomery, have flown in from the United States to take the pictures and write the words for this book.

Though it's only our first day together, we're all eager to see a tapir—especially since it will soon be dark. The setting sun is a salmon pink ball beneath a bank of lavender clouds.

"Some of the most beautiful sunsets in the world are in the Pantanal," says Pati, "and tonight—"

RAP-RAP-RAP!

"Tapir! Tapir! Tapir!" Pati whispers excitedly. This time she's sure.

We hush. The crinkling songs of frogs and insects fill the silence.

Ahead we see our quarry. The animal

looks as big as a rhino—though it really isn't. A rhino can weigh as much as a car; a lowland tapir weighs about as much as three fat passengers. Still, the tapir is South America's largest terrestrial mammal, bigger than its biggest cats—the slinky spotted jaguar and the stealthy sand-colored puma. It's an impressive, powerful beast.

The tapir stands about three hundred yards ahead of us, just to the right of the sandy track. It stays perfectly still for a full minute. Then it trots across. José and Gabriel leap from the open back of the truck. Gabriel carries the dart gun; José's job is to instruct him on how to keep track of the tapir, or herd the tapir toward him if necessary. They chase after the big animal, hunched over in a running crouch. Soon dusk swallows them from sight.

Pati folds her slender hands in her lap to wait.

We listen to the three-noted, upward-trending whistle of the grouselike bird known here as the Jaó. Its voice sounds like a person asking a question—as we are, silently, while we wait. How many tapirs live in this area? Do any have babies? Do young tapirs grow up to live in the same area where they were born, or do they move far away? But as the seconds tick into minutes, the insistent whistle of the Jaó seems to be voicing our most urgent question: Will we be able to catch a tapir to find out?

Meet the Tapir Team

PATRICIA MEDICI: team leader, age thirty-eight
NATIONALITY: Brazilian
LANGUAGES: Portuguese, English, Spanish

The day after she graduated from the University of São Paulo, Pati found herself driving to a remote forest where she would oversee eight field assistants studying nine different groups of tiny black monkeys. All of Pati's assistants were men. She later found out that they had a bet among them that she wouldn't be strong enough to do the job.

They lost the bet—but gained a friend, and a place in conservation history. Thanks to the work of Pati's organization in Brazil (the Instituto de Pesquisas Ecológicas), rare black lion tamarins—tiny long-tailed primates with fluffy manes and silky black hair—are no longer in immediate danger of extinction. Pati oversaw the first successful effort to move groups of these miniature monkeys from an area threatened by logging to a different, safer forest, proving that the endangered animals could not only survive, but thrive after a move.

Pati found tapirs even more tempting than tamarins. She started studying them for her Ph.D. thesis (which she wrote in her second language, English!) in Brazil's Atlantic Forest, a green, moist, but rapidly shrinking habitat. In twelve years of study there, Pati managed to radio-collar twenty-five tapirs. The tapirs were extremely shy, and with good reason: eaten by jaguars and pumas, hunted by people with guns, and often killed by cars, they were also threatened by the timber, cattle, and charcoal industries that were chewing away at their forest home. Pati's work in the Atlantic Forest was the first long-term study of lowland tapirs in the world. But as she points out, "Tapirs live in lots of very different kinds of places. They live in high mountains. They live in the Amazon. Tapirs live in four different biomes [major habitat types] just in Brazil alone! So we knew that to make recommendations for conservation in the other places where they live, we needed to go to each of these places."

For Pati, the vast and beautiful Pantanal was the next stop on the tapir trail.

José Maria de Aragão: field assistant, age forty-six
Nationality: Brazilian
Language: Portuguese

José (Joe-ZAY) grew up on a small farm where his dad worked as a helper. He and his dad, stepmother, and four younger siblings lived in a hand-built wooden house with no electricity. For fun, he liked to hunt birds with slingshots and spears and build traps for small animals. Through fourth grade, all the farm workers' kids went to a one-room schoolhouse with a single teacher. When José was twelve, his parents sent him to a school in the city, and when he was in eighth grade, he quit school to start working. "But he never lost his thirst for learning," says Pati.

José worked at various jobs (one was as a mechanic's assistant at a sugar cane mill) until he was hired by an animal rescue league that was trying to capture and move wild animals—monkeys, snakes, armadillos—that would otherwise be drowned when a hydro-electric project flooded their forest. He used his childhood trapping experience to rescue animals instead of kill them. He loved the work. "Capturing animals is really exciting," he told me in Portuguese as Gabriel translated, "because each individual animal is different. And it's more fun helping them than killing them." He was so good at trapping that when the rescue project was done, IPÊ hired him as a field assistant for the black lion tamarin project—and Pati made sure to hire him again when she began studying tapirs. "I hope he never retires," says Pati. "I don't know what I would do without him!" José and his wife live in Teodoro Sampaio in the state of São Paulo, where they raised two daughters. The younger girl is Pati's goddaughter, and at the recent wedding of the older daughter, Pati was the bride's maid of honor.

DOROTHÉE ORDONNEAU, *zoo veterinarian, age thirty-one*
NATIONALITY: French
LANGUAGES: French, English

Dorothée wanted to be a veterinarian since she was five years old. "But to spend my whole life with only cows and dogs would be a pity," she said, "because there are so many species!" Growing up, she imagined living in a rainforest among monkeys. Today she's living both dreams. At her zoo in France she works with every species in the collection, from tapirs to zebras, from snakes to birds. And she also works in the wild, volunteering on projects like this one. When she gets done with the tapirs, she and her boyfriend—also a veterinarian—are going to help with a project in Madagascar, the big island off the east coast of southern Africa, studying lemurs, the most primitive primates of all.

At the home the couple share in the small French village of Barville, one whole room is devoted to aquariums for colorful, tropical poison-dart frogs. Dorothée also lives with a dog, and (outside) three alpacas (they look like hairy camels without humps), and about 150,000 honeybees.

GABRIEL DAMASCENO: darting specialist, age thirty-four
NATIONALITY: American and Brazilian
LANGUAGES: Portuguese, Spanish, English

Born in San Diego, California, to a Brazilian dad who is a chemist and an American mom who was earning her doctorate in languages, Gabriel grew up loving travel, languages, music, animals, and nature. His father was a hunter and outdoorsman. His godfather, a shooting instructor, gave Gabriel his first shotgun when he was twelve. A fine shot at target practice, he went on his first real hunt at fourteen. He shot six pigeons, but one of them was only wounded; he tried to wring its neck to put it out of its misery, but it wouldn't die. He had to hand the suffering bird over to his dad to kill it. "That was my first hunt and my last," he says. Gabriel was taught that "if you kill it, you eat it." But that night, as he was cleaning the birds at home, he lost his appetite—for his meal and for hunting.

Darting with a tranquilizer gun, though, "has all the excitement and adrenaline of a hunt, but you don't hurt the animal—you're helping advance knowledge of the species and trying to help them out!" A "self-taught tinkerer," Gabriel sews his own camouflage outfits and designs much of his own gear—including a system for shooting biopsy darts to take tiny skin samples from the giant otters (they grow six feet long from head to tail) that his girlfriend studies elsewhere in the Pantanal. He reels the darts back in on fishing line.

Gabriel is also a musician. For twenty years he was a professional drummer, specializing in the African-influenced Brazilian music called samba. He named his favorite iguana (who grew three feet long and learned to use a potty in the bathroom) Conga, after the Latin American drum.

EDUARDO MORENO: veterinarian, epidemiologist (an expert on public health and on outbreaks of disease among animals), age twenty-eight
NATIONALITY: Brazilian
LANGUAGES: Portuguese, English

Eduardo always loved animals. But growing up in an apartment in the southern Brazilian city of Londrina with his parents and brother, he wasn't allowed to adopt a dog, and he couldn't keep any of the stray cats he constantly brought home. As a boy, he dreamed of being a vet, but in Brazil, the usual study program for a veterinary degree concentrates on food animals. He wanted to help animals live—not help raise them for slaughter. "So," he said, "I shaped my own career."

He took the usual veterinary courses in college, but he also studied biology, human health, conservation, and ecology. He even studied global positioning satellites at Brazil's National Institute for Space Research. ("My mother couldn't understand why I was in space training!" he said.)

The reason? Combining all these disciplines, Eduardo was training to become a veterinary epidemiologist (epuh-deemy-OL-ogist), a specialist in the ecology of animal disease outbreaks. "How disease is transmitted can be complicated," he says, "and so many factors can be important. Even the wind can bring disease." (How? One way: wind might blow in disease-carrying birds or mosquitoes.) Eduardo's job is to unravel and understand all these contributing factors in order to stop an outbreak of disease—or prevent it from happening in the first place.

On the tapir team, Eduardo is particularly interested in studying parasites, bacteria, viruses, and fungi in tapirs—especially diseases they may have gotten from cattle, horses, or pigs. If domestic animals' disease organisms show up in the tapirs' blood or poop, does that mean the tapirs are sick? Maybe not. Eduardo loves solving mysteries like that.

"Work here is not like working," he says. "It's not easy—but it's fun, too!"

Gabriel returns to the Land Cruiser
after an exhausting search.

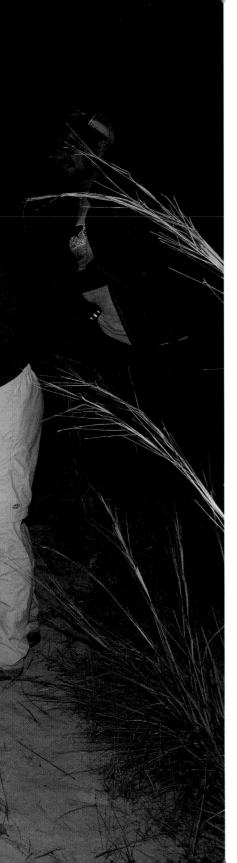

CHAPTER 2
Tapir Trials

We hold the quiet like a prayer for the next seven minutes. And then we see the men coming back.

"It was a female. An adult with a whitish face," Gabriel tells us. "She ran into the thorny brush . . ." With thick, tough skin, tapirs can bash through the most tangled scrub. But there was no way the two men could follow her.

We drive on. José swings his powerful spotlight toward the trees and grass lining the edges of a baía (buy-EE-uh), a natural drainage area that changes with the rainfall from a lake (as this one was last May) to a giant puddle (as many of them are now, in August). We see a pair of crab-eating foxes hunting small rodents in the grass. The female jogs ahead and stops; her suitor circles around and makes a chirping sound, and she swivels her ears forward. A six-banded armadillo scuttles by. In the distance we see the reddish eye shine of one of the Pantanal's four species of deer, the pampas deer. Fireflies drift by like tiny, lazy comets.

We're desperate to see a tapir—but for the moment, we'll settle for hearing about some. As Pati drives, we ask Dorothée to tell us about the tapirs at her zoo in France.

When Dorothée first joined the zoo staff, the tapirs, Leticia and Papyrus, were among her favorite animals. Dorothée particularly loved Leticia, and the feeling was mutual. In exchange for a nice long scratch and a treat such as an apple or zucchini, Leticia even let Dorothée give her eye drops when she had an eye infection. Leticia and her mate had tried but failed to produce babies. Dorothée quickly discovered that Leticia had an infection in her womb. Dorothée cured it, and fourteen months later (that's how long it takes to make a baby tapir), Cali, a little female, dark brown with white stripes and spots, was born.

Leticia and her first calf, Cali. All species of tapirs—even the black and white Malayan tapir—have spots and stripes as babies.

Oscar stands in the doorway to his stall.

Two years after Cali came a son, Oscar. "Both so small!" said Dorothée. "Six kilos!" (a little over thirteen pounds). The tapir calves were the stars of the zoo. "The children at the zoo go crazy to see the baby. They say it looks like a watermelon," said Dorothée. "They love the funny nose. That cracks them up."

In captivity, tapirs can be gentle and affectionate. Back in the mid-1800s a European explorer in Burma met a man who kept a Malayan tapir as a pet. "It was a very inoffensive animal and became as much domesticated as a cat," reported a British major, MacFarquhar. "It followed its master round the compound like a dog, but looked as unseemly as a hog."

Gerald Durrell, the author and adventuring zookeeper, caught a tapir in Argentina. He named him Claudius "because," he wrote, "with that Roman snout of his he looks like one of the ancient emperors." Claudius tamely wandered the garden surrounding Durrell's hostess's house (until he got thrown out for eating her prized flowers).

When Pati visits zoos around the world, she's often invited to pet and scratch tapirs. They particularly enjoy a belly rub. But Pati knows that any tapir is a powerful animal that can turn dangerous if threatened. In a zoo in Oklahoma, a visitor asked a keeper to stand between a mother tapir and her baby for a picture. Bad idea.

The mother attacked, sinking her teeth so deep into the keeper's neck that she tore out the vocal cords, then bit and pulled her arm. The keeper now uses an artificial voice box and an artificial arm.

The story of the accident helps us appreciate the tapir's strength and bravery. Now, as we drive on, Pati says, "We're getting close to one of our areas with traps." In addition to trying to dart any tapirs we encounter, Pati and José have set up ten box traps—wood and wire enclosures, each about the size of a horse stall, baited with salt, which tapirs love. When the hooves of a tapir strike a stick in front of the salt trough, it triggers the trapdoor to fall shut, safely capturing the tapir inside. Maybe a tapir is investigating one of those traps right now. "We should be quiet," whispers Pati, "because we don't want to disturb—"

RAP-RAP-RAP!

Pati sticks her head out the window to confer with José. "Two! There's *two!*" she whispers to us. "Great!"

Gabriel and José leap from the car, and we watch their flashlights dart through the tall grass. Dorothée quietly unzips Pati's backpack and removes a radio collar to ready it for the tapir. Eduardo holds the spotlight to help the men in the field. Frog songs pulse and jingle from the shallow basin nearby as the moon rises, nearly full—a big white eye staring down at the Pantanal, as if it alone understands the great wetland's mysteries.

Again, we wait. To avoid the noise of opening the car door, Pati snakes her slender body out the driver's window to whisper in Portuguese to Eduardo in the back of the vehicle. Pati notices that what they see is a mother and a juvenile. If she could collar the mom, she could follow them both!

Finally, at 6:52 p.m.: "Ay-yi-yi!" whispers Eduardo. We see Gabriel and José coming back.

"I had her in my sights," Gabriel tells us, frustrated. "I was twenty-five meters [about twenty-seven yards] away. So close. It was perfect . . ."

The men are dripping with sweat. Though this evening is a comfortable 75 degrees or so, Gabriel and José are hot and sweaty from running bent over through the tall grass so as not to frighten the tapirs. Gabriel works hard to stay hidden. Not only does he design and sew his own camouflage field clothes— he even designed a floppy camo hat with a zippered brim, from which he can release a beekeeper's veil in case he's attacked by bees on the job!—he never wears insect repellent or chews gum or smokes cigarettes or sucks candy, because the smell might give him away. That's also why he crops his hair short (he seldom has to shampoo) and breathes through his nose, not his mouth, even though that's hard to do at a running crouch with a four-hundred-pound mother tapir and her baby near enough to dart.

Gabriel said that for most of the pursuit he could hear the tapirs but not see them. He rushed forward anyway. Then he spotted the mother through his rifle's infrared night scope—and she was thrillingly close. She would have been an easy shot. But she was at the wrong angle. "You want to approach at a ninety-degree angle," he explained, in order to hit the fleshiest part of the animal, above the hind leg. Instead, he was at a forty-five-degree angle, too far in back of her. He couldn't be sure the dart would hit the right place. He might hurt the mother. Rather than risk it, he let them go.

The men are disappointed. But Pati says, "It's great just to get a chance to even see the tapirs. That's fantastic!"

This is only our first night together since Nic and I joined the team; the others arrived three days earlier, mainly to set the traps and organize two truckloads of gear: veterinary and scientific equipment and supplies, laptops for entering data, petrol for the two vehicles, salt to bait the tapirs, building materials if the traps need repair, clothing, sunscreen, and bug repellent for two weeks. Tomorrow is our first full day together. We can hardly wait till morning—and it won't be long.

Life on the Fazenda

At Baía das Pedras, where Pati conducts her study, cattle and wild animals live side by side, as they have lived for two hundred years.

The first ranchers who came to the Pantanal really couldn't do it any other way. Nature had the upper hand. They couldn't kill all the wild animals even if they wanted to, and the area was too vast for the first few ranchers to drain or raze. Instead, the people and their domestic animals had to learn to adapt to this changeable new place.

That's what Rita (pronounced "HEE-tah") Jurgielewicz's grandparents did when they became early pioneers in this corner of the Pantanal and established this cattle ranch, or *fazenda* (fah-ZEN-dah), in 1896.

Ranching in the Pantanal is different from ranching anywhere else, said Rita's husband, Carlos, while the couple's son, Vicente, a veterinarian, translated his father's Portuguese to English. Raising cattle here really only works in partnership with nature. And unlike at other ranches, where cattlemen hunt down and kill the native creatures, thinking it makes more room for cattle, Rita and Carlos let these animals thrive—even the pumas. They don't fell the trees to try to make every inch a pasture. They don't replace the native plants with exotic grasses. They're dedicated to running their *fazenda* in the traditional *Pantaneiro* style. Working with nature, "we've found a way that's worked for two hundred years," Carlos said.

Wise ranching is one reason tapirs thrive in the Pantanal, says Pati. In other areas, tapirs are disappearing because people hunt them for meat. Not here. There's no shortage of meat on a ranch (Brazilians are the third-largest consumers of beef in the world, and the world's second-largest producer of it). Anyone who gets the urge to hunt goes for the wild pigs, whose ancestors were brought here by Europeans and are now considered pests. Tapirs elsewhere are hit by cars—again not a problem here, where the roads are dirt and cars drive slowly. And Baía das Pedras has another plus for tapirs. For some reason, though jaguars live elsewhere in the Pantanal, they don't live here, only pumas. One less predator for a tapir to worry about.

Rita and Carlos raise 5,000 cattle, 200 horses, 120 sheep, and dozens of chickens, goats, and pigs at Baía das Pedras. (Rita's brother, Jocy, and sister, Solange, own neighboring *fazendas*.) Eight cowboys, or *Pantaneiros*, work on the ranch to help them—sometimes more during busy times. The cowboys start their day at 4:00 a.m., milking the dairy cows that provide the ranch with milk for drinking and for delicious homemade cheese. After breakfast, on horseback, they get back to work. They move the cattle from pasture to pasture, oversee the births of the calves, and vaccinate and brand the cattle. Riding along the dusty dirt road on their hardy *Pantaneiro* horses, they "drive" all the cattle—thousands at once—the thirty miles to market in Río Negro. In the wet season, when there is less to do, the cowboys fix fences and repair equipment. They make new saddles from the hides of ranch cows and weave saddle blankets from the wool of the sheep.

Of course, the Jurgielewiczes have modernized since Rita's grandfather's time. Electricity came in 2003 (they're the last *fazenda* on the line from Campo Grande to have it—the others beyond are still waiting). Before that, they used noisy generators to power

A cowboy rounds up
cattle to be branded.

Maté, a tea made from local herbs, is sipped from a cow's horn.

lights and sometimes fans from about 5:00 to 9:00 p.m. But thanks to electricity, they could add a new business to the ranch: tourism. Each year, some three hundred people come from around the world to stay at the ranch and see the amazing wildlife of the Pantanal. Tourism sounds like a big change, but really, it, too, continues a family tradition. Rita's grandparents and parents were famous for their hospitality. (They named the place after the stones—pedras—that made one of the wetlands passable to oxcarts so people could easily visit. Without the stones, the oxcarts would sink in the mud.) Rita's parents held big dances and barbeques. They loved to make new friends, just as Rita and Carlos do today. Visitors typically come for the wildlife, but many of them fall in love with the *Pantaneiro* lifestyle as well.

The cowboys make their own lassos, saddles, and other equipment from ranch materials.

Vicente said that the *fazenda* was a great place for a kid to grow up. When he was five, his favorite game with was playing rancher with his two younger sisters. They made houses and fences out of sticks and used rocks or oranges as pretend animals.

One day around Christmas, young Vicente and his sisters Izabel and Júlia told their mom that they wished their house had colorful holiday lights like the ones in the city. That night, Rita drove them to a *baía* on the property. She shone a spotlight into the water. The *baía* glowed with hundreds of red balls—the reflecting eyes of crowds of crocodiles, the Pantanal's famous yacare caimans. It was more thrilling and beautiful than any electric Christmas display the city could offer.

The yacare caiman eats snails and fish, especially enjoying piranhas. It also preys on birds and mammals.

Doves flying at sunset.

CHAPTER 3
Tapir Traps

We rise at 4:00 a.m., swigging strong Brazilian coffee for energy. Good thing we're staying at the pretty, orange-painted cement house here at Baía das Pedras. We're lucky that the owners, Rita and Carlos, help support Pati's study; they love tapirs and other wild animals and are eager to learn more about them. Here, the team sleeps in comfy beds, takes hot showers, and eats hearty meals prepared by the same friendly staff that often welcomes tourists. We're fortified for a long day ahead.

Though tapirs are sometimes out and about by day, they're most active at dusk, dark, and dawn. Early morning is an ideal time to spot them. We're hoping for darting success before we start to check the box traps. Pati tells us that we'll wait to check the traps till 8:00 a.m. because up to that time, tapirs might still be approaching them.

The traps have been very successful. All but three of the nine tapirs Pati and her team have radio collared here since her study began three years ago were caught in box traps. "Darting is very difficult compared to trapping," Pati explains. One of the darted tapirs, an elderly male, was named Bandaid— because after he was darted, he ran into the thorny brush and everyone needed bandages

With radio telemetry and binoculars, José and Pati search for one of the collared tapirs.

for all the cuts they got before they finally collared him!

"The reason this method is so hard is that the tapirs already see and hear you," Pati continues. "But it's an important complement to the traps." By actively searching the landscape instead of just waiting for a tapir to trip a trap, "you get an idea of tapir hot spots. You see social interactions, like whether a female has a baby or is traveling with a male." For instance, one female, Kelly, darted and captured in 2009, was later seen in the company of a male—whom the team then darted, collared, and named Benjamin Martlet. "And possibly, darting is less stressful for the tapir," Pati says, since the animal doesn't have to wait in a trap. "But darting is dangerous. And it's more stressful for *us!*"

Pati goes out with a team about once a month during the dry season, and not all expeditions have the same focus: sometimes she concentrates on following tapirs with radio collars or collecting and analyzing the animals' dung; other times she spends much of her time visiting rural schools, telling kids about the importance of conservation. But on this particular expedition Pati's top priority is radio collaring more tapirs. The nine tapirs she's already collared might sound like enough, but four collars either fell off or stopped working. (One transmitter, on a healthy young male named Vivek Tudor, either died or fell off without ever revealing a single location. Frustratingly, no one has seen Vivek Tudor since.) Bandaid died of old age in 2010 (his radio collar helped her find his

body). That leaves only four—and eventually Pati would like to collar as many as twenty.

Just eleven minutes after we pile into the grumbling old Toyota, we see our first tapir. Gabriel and José leap from the car; Pati grabs her notebook and her global positioning satellite (GPS) unit (connecting with orbiting satellites, the device gives our location in longitude and latitude). Pati always notes the time, place, and weather when we've seen a tapir. But again, we're disappointed: Gabriel and José come back soon. The tapir was a handsome adult male, but he ran away.

"We'll go back to the same place where we saw the two tapirs last night," Pati says. By 5:35 a.m. we've arrived. The Toyota is running rough and noisy. Perhaps we'll have better luck on foot. We get out to walk.

With the engine off, the voices of the Pantanal swell around us. With the dawning light, nighttime's frog calls fade to the morning songs of birds. The *Jaó* birds' whistles are joined by the twinkling calls of parakeets. The pheasantlike chackalaka's voice sounds like a monkey and carries more than a mile.

The flightless rhea is related to the ostrich of Africa. It stands about four feet tall and can run at speeds of thirty-five miles per hour.

The curicaca, a water bird with a curved bill and long orange legs, duets with his mate. Local people say these birds seem to be screaming at each other, with machine-gun rapidity, *"Quero morrer!" "Quero matar!"* The Portuguese translates to "I wanna die!" "I wanna kill!" ("That pair must have been married too long," whispers Eduardo.)

The Pantanal is a bird lover's paradise. The sky blushes pink with flocks of roseate spoonbills. On the ground, a seriema, a tall bird with a crest of feathers that looks like messy hair, prances by. (It's one of the few birds with eyelashes.) Wading birds with long toes stride across lily pads, and sixty-pound ostrichlike rheas run instead of fly. At least 470 different kinds of birds have been recorded in the Pantanal, from toucans and macaws to storks as tall as a man. One expert boasted of seeing 196 species of birds in a twenty-four-hour period.

It's 5:45 a.m. *"Anta!"* José whispers the Brazilian Portuguese word for tapir. (The word *tapir* comes from the native Tupi people of the Amazon.) Pati motions us to drop to our knees in the sand while José and Gabriel sneak ahead.

Alas, soon they come walking back. Another false alarm. The "tapir" was a feral pig.

But as we continue along the sandy track, Pati warns, "We have to be very quiet right now. This is tapir land." The sand cushions the sound of our hiking boots. Maybe we'll sneak up on a tapir after all.

Toco toucans have the largest beaks, relative to their body size, of any bird. They eat fruit and small animals.

Six-banded armadillos are common in the Pantanal. They are good diggers, and they run for the cover of their burrows when alarmed.

We come upon our own boot prints from yesterday. Now there are other tracks on top of them. Tapirs! The tracks are shaped almost like maple leaves, with three or four pointy, hoofed toes and a smaller, roughly triangular heel pad. The footprints of the ancestors of almost all hoofed beasts looked much like this millions of years ago—even those of horses, who have just one toe on each foot today. But when these animals were just evolving, each foot had lots of toes. (In the Eocene, thirty-five million years ago, early horses had five toes on each foot; by the Miocene, they still had three.)

We're near a pasture fence, and we can see one of Pati's traps in the morning light. The door is open—no tapir yet. But there are several ways to catch a tapir, and along this track Pati wants to set a different kind of trap: a camera trap to capture images.

Once it is activated by motion (any passing object will trigger it—they get lots of pictures of other animals), the digital camera takes five photos in rapid-fire succession. Why five? "That way you not only get the tapir's face, but you can often get the back end to tell if it's male or female," Pati explains. "And if there's another tapir with it, the photo will show that too"—along with the date, time, temperature, and phase of the moon. Thanks to these digital pictures, thousands of which can be downloaded from a single flash drive, you can tell if one tapir passed by and, two minutes later, another followed—or if one came running from the opposite direction (perhaps chased by another tapir. Sometimes males fight over females). José lashes a camouflaged Reconyx Semi-Covert camera to a fence post, just at tapir height, and turns it on.

We stop for breakfast at 7:15 a.m.— apples; small, sweet bananas; and plain cookies. We've not caught a tapir, but "with ten traps to check," says Pati, "there's a good chance."

The third trap we'll check today, she says, is our best bet. Just three months earlier, on separate days, this particular trap captured Benjamin Martlet again—he got a new radio collar—and a new female who was named Morena, in honor of Eduardo.

"Best only one person checks the trap, so as not to leave human scent," says Pati. We wait nearby, but she returns quickly. "No tapir—but plenty of tapir tracks around!"

At 7:45 a.m. we check a second trap. Tracks, but no tapir.

The sandy trail leading to the third trap looks promising. Pati points out the fresh tapir footprints and even fresh tapir poop (sort of like miniature horse droppings). "This area has really good plants for tapirs," Pati says. Like their relatives, horses and rhinos, tapirs are plant eaters. In addition to fruit, tapirs eat many different types of leaves. Tapir moms and their babies especially like to hide in strips of forest like the one we enter now, with acuri palms laden with bunches of green fruit and fig trees with twisting roots that seem to flow like candle wax.

But the forest has something else, too, as we discover once we emerge. Dorothée has what looks like a patch of gray lint stuck to the legs of her trousers. But it's not lint.

"Ew!" she says looking down. *Ticks!*

There are hundreds of them, each smaller than the head of a pin. When they bite, they leave a red, itchy welt. "It's impossible not to get them," Eduardo tells us, pulling up his shirt to reveal dozens of red welts. "Now you can say you have been to the Pantanal." Luckily, these ticks don't carry diseases that infect people, so we don't have to worry about Lyme disease or Rocky Mountain spotted fever.

After a short walk along the sandy track, it's back to the forest. Again we try to brush away ticks by the hundreds. "Now we're really close," Pati says quietly. She motions for us to wait while she goes ahead.

José finds fresh tapir prints.

She returns with thumbs up and a brilliant smile. "It's a tapir!" Pati's thrilled—but worried, too. The tapir, a male, was standing on his hind legs, pawing at the wood-and-wire trap, trying to escape. She backed away quickly before she scared him even more. Above all, she doesn't want the tapir to hurt himself.

Pati explains the procedure ahead: Eduardo and Dorothée will tranquilize the tapir. Once he's sedated, the rest of us will approach. Pati and José will climb inside the trap with the tapir first and put on the radio collar. Pati will record the data. Dorothée will help take skin and blood samples. Gabriel will film the event.

Though it's only 8:30 a.m., our shirts are plastered to our skin from the heat. Or is it the excitement? José and Pati go ahead to take another, more careful look. We hope the tapir has calmed down.

Pati returns with the news: "It's either Luis Uruguaio or Felippe Lion!" How can she tell? He's already got a collar! "Only Luis and Felippe have black collars like this," she says. Both adult males were captured and collared in May of last year, within days of each other, in the same trap in another part of the ranch. But which tapir is this?

Pati can tell with the turn of a dial on the telemetry receiver. Each tapir has its own channel because each radio collar sends out a unique signal. If you want to find Felippe, tune in your receiver to channel .08, and if he's anywhere nearby, a soft kissing sound will come from the device. It gets louder when you swing the antenna in the direction of the animal. Luis's channel is .15.

The signal is loud and clear. It's Felippe—and Pati is delighted. She'd been wondering where he was. "He spends most of his time on the other side of the *baía*, in the neighboring ranch," she says. "Our telemetry tells us he only comes here to Baía das Pedras in the driest part of the season. Maybe we'll get his first camera-trap photo!"

Since Felippe was captured recently, there's no need to sedate him or take samples. While the rest of us hide behind trees to watch, José stands on top of the trap to heave open the door. Felippe stands stock-still. We get a close-up look at a magnificent wild tapir: we can see the light stripes and spots on his legs. Elsewhere in South America, lowland tapirs lose these markings as adults, but not in the Pantanal. We admire the white tips of his ears. For nearly fifteen minutes, only one ear moves. Then he lifts his splendid, flexible nose, exposing pink gums and white front teeth, and he spreads his nostrils. We can almost hear him wondering: Is it true? Am I free at last?

When he finally departs, he does so with the grace and power of a horse. Felippe gallops out of the enclosure, crashes through the underbrush, and is gone in an instant.

There were tapir tracks near some of the other traps that morning, but no more tapirs inside. So after a hearty late lunch back at the ranch, Pati suggests we head out on foot.

At 4:30 p.m. the worst of the day's heat has passed, as the birds well know. The electric blue hyacinth macaws are starting to fly back to their palm tree roosts. The black and white jabiru storks no longer need to shade their nestlings beneath outstretched eight-foot wings. Ahead of us on the track, on a golden stalk, perches a red fireball of a bird: a vermilion flycatcher. He's so beautiful some of us can't help crying out, "Oh!"

"Guys, let's turn the volume down," says Gabriel. He's intent on darting a tapir, upset that three already got away. We resume our silent single-file walk. Soon we are rewarded. At 5:10 p.m. we see a long shape lying sphinxlike in the track ahead. We approach slowly until we are perhaps only a hundred yards away . . . from a puma!

Felippe bolts for freedom.

Once he became aware of our presence, the puma slunk back into the trees.

The fer-de-lance's venom causes severe bleeding and destroys muscle tissue. The biologist Clodomiro Picado described a bite victim as having to watch his body "becoming a corpse piece by piece."

José rolls up his sleeve and shows me his arm. It's covered in goose flesh. The tawny cat, a predator capable of killing a tapir, is intently watching something off to our left. His long tail, as thick as a child's arm, flicks back and forth like a cat watching a mouse. And in fact, we have stumbled upon a really big cat-and-mouse game. The 100- to 250-pound puma is watching a family of capybaras, the world's largest rodents, who can grow to 140 pounds. On our knees, we watch the cat for ten minutes. When we try to creep closer, he turns toward us in a crouch and stares at us for a moment with golden eyes. He turns to trot briskly into a strip of forest.

We walk on past sunset and into the night. A full moon rises. Still no tapir. When we turn back, at 7:30 p.m., we're tired. By the time we see the lights of the ranch, some of us are stumbling, sometimes kicking the round, dark mounds on the ground. We don't need our flashlights to know they're just dried cow poop and they won't even soil our shoes.

That's when Nic sees it, just eight inches from Pati's foot: another round, dark mound. But this is no cowpat. It's a fer-de-lance, perhaps the deadliest snake in South America, coiled in the strike position. As it vibrates its tail, trying to warn us away, we step back in awe.

The Two Benjamins

"I love tapirs," the fifth-grader wrote Pati on his e-mail from his London boarding school, "and I want to help you with tapir conservation."

Benjamin Brind had fallen in love with tapirs when he did a project on them in fifth grade. During his research he discovered Pati and her work. With his e-mail in 2008, Benjamin began a friendship with Pati that continues to this day.

Pati wrote back, and after consulting with his parents, the following year, when Benjamin was twelve, he and Pati hatched a plan across the ocean to raise money for Pati's new tapir project in the Pantanal.

Benjamin's school, Westminster Under School, always holds a summer "fete" day during the last week of the term. While fathers and sons play a cricket match (the British national sport, a little like baseball), the students at the boys' school run some thirty different stalls, selling chances to play different games, from basketball toss to snail races. Parents man another ten booths, selling everything from plants to cakes. Each year at a special assembly, the students are invited to make presentations about the charities they'd like the next year's sales to benefit.

"I think it's time that the under school supported a charity which helps animals," Benjamin told his audience, "since we are destroying their world and they cannot speak up for themselves." He spoke about tapirs and about Pati's work in Brazil. And then he showed a one-minute video filmed at Pati's study site. A tapir looked into the camera, stretched forth its glorious, flexible trunk, and flared its nostrils. "Awwww!" cried the audience. The other kids were hooked.

The next day, when the school voted for their favorite charities, Pati's project won more votes than the other five charities in the competition. Thanks to Benjamin, the fete raised more than 1,600 British pounds that year—the equivalent of more than $2,000—for Pati's project. His donation covered the cost of a field expedition in 2010, including transportation of the entire tapir team to the ranch, fuel for two weeks, and all field supplies.

And that's how some of the collared tapirs in Pati's study got their last names. Sonia Westminster's last name honors Benjamin's school. Four other tapirs have last names borrowed from the school's dormitories: Fleury, Tudor, Lion, and Martlet. But Benjamin himself is especially honored: his is the first name Pati bestowed on the handsome young male she discovered consorting with the tapir named Kelly, just months after Benjamin's school fete concluded. "Benjamin Martlet is one of my favorite tapirs, for sure!" says Pati.

Back in England, the human Benjamin is now a teenager contemplating college. And he still keeps up with Pati and his tapir namesake in Brazil.

Benjamin, photographed after his first capture in 2009.

The team prepares to collar
the first tapir of the day.

CHAPTER 4
Tapir Overload

Four a.m. comes quickly, and we're traveling by 4:30. We're planning to return to the place where we saw the first tapir yesterday. Mindful of the snake, we're going by car.

Along the way, we pass one of Pati's traps. The door is down!

José leaps out of the Land Cruiser. He's back almost instantly: "*Anta!*" he says.

"I hope it's not Benjamin," Pati says under her breath.

Though Benjamin Martlet is one of her favorite tapirs, she doesn't want to see him in the trap. Just hours before Nic and I joined the expedition, the team had caught him in one of the traps. They were delighted because his radio collar had again fallen off and they were eager to replace it, but they couldn't get Benjamin to go to sleep. They tried for more than an hour and darted him three different times. He never even got drowsy. They're still wondering why.

Pati accompanies José to the trap to see who's been caught.

"It's a juvenile," Pati reports. "He's going to grow, so we can't put a radio collar on him. But we can do something new." On this expedition, for the first time, the team will be equipping tapirs with microchips—the same sort of identification device vets in the United States use on pet dogs and cats. A microchip won't fall off. Encased in a smooth capsule the size of a grain of rice, a silicon microchip is attached to a tuning capacitor and a copper antenna coil. The chip holds the information—a special ID number. By using a handheld scanner much like those at store checkout counters, a biologist or vet energizes the capacitor, which activates the microchip to send its ID number out through the antenna coil and into the scanner's display screen. Using a device that looks like a big stapler, a vet can insert the chip beneath the skin with less pain than a vaccination.

José and Eduardo dart the juvenile tapir.

The young tapir kicks inside the trap like an anxious horse in a stall. The team goes to work, readying all the gear they'll need. Most important is the anesthetic dart. Eduardo opens his medical kit. Kneeling in the grass, he fills the syringe with tranquilizer drugs.

In her notebook, Pati notes the time: 5:54 a.m.; the date; the weather; the trap location. Eduardo and Dorothée unpack and carefully lay out the supplies: tape measure; surgical gloves; a green bandana decorated with peace signs to cover the tapir's eyes (to protect the eyes and keep him calm, since the eyes stay open during sedation). Vials, syringes, antiseptic spray. They label vials in Magic Marker that will hold samples: *pêlo* (fur) and *pele* (skin). The genetic material in these samples will show which tapirs are related to each other.

The medical kit is extensive. It holds the sedative and its antidote, as well as other medicines, in case something goes wrong. Eduardo and Dorothée are ready with drugs to stimulate the heart and to resuscitate breathing. The two vets will be on opposite sides of the walls of the tapir trap. Dorothée will pass supplies to Eduardo. They will speak in English, a second language for both of them, as Dorothée speaks no Portuguese and Eduardo speaks no French.

6:15 a.m.: It's light now; the bird chorus is loud and the mosquitoes ferocious. "Ready to go?" asks Pati.

José, kneeling to insert his dart pistol through an opening in the box trap, shoots the drug into the tapir's rump.

6:30 a.m.: As the rest of us wait out of sight, we hear the tapir kick the boards of the trap. Why isn't he asleep?

"We are thinking there is something wrong with the dart," Gabriel suggests. When the dart stops its forward motion after hitting the tapir, a firing pin inside the dart is supposed to continue forward, injecting the drug. Perhaps, for some reason, it didn't. It seems to have delivered no sedative at all.

"We'll have to try again," Pati says. Eduardo fills another dart with the sedative drug.

6:45 a.m.: José fires the dart pistol again. Five jabiru storks fly overhead. The wind in their huge wings sounds like a faraway jet.

7:02 a.m.: Eduardo inspects the tapir. "The dart didn't work," he says. He pulls the dart out and shows us: the shaft is broken, and at least some of the drug has leaked out. Possibly some was injected—maybe enough to sedate the tapir. We'll have to wait and see. A dove gives its slow, lonely call. A big black curassow makes a sound like a person blowing across a bottle top.

7:15 a.m.: We've been here an hour. We should be finished by now, but we haven't even started. A curicaca couple duets, screaming (in Portuguese), "I wanna die!" "I wanna kill!"

"That's what Pati is probably thinking right now," Gabriel says.

Pati decides to try a third dart. This time she asks José to increase the pressure of the dart pistol. If the firing pin is at fault, maybe the pressure will help drive it forward within the dart to inject the drug.

7:35 a.m.: "The tapir is still awake," Pati reports. What's the problem? Is this a repeat of what happened when they tried to sedate Benjamin?

A syringe is used to dispense sedative.

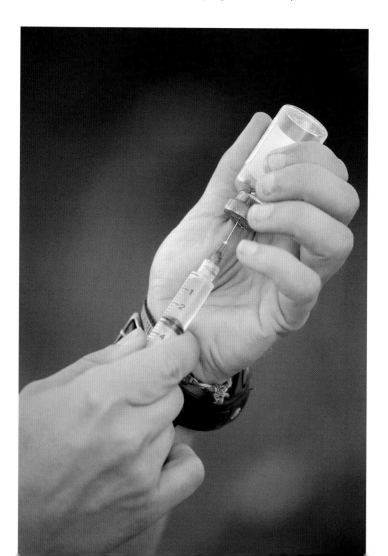

On the road to unraveling the mysteries of tapirs, Pati and the team must first solve the puzzle of what's wrong with the equipment. The gun could be misfiring, not delivering enough pressure. The dart could be defective. The mechanism that propels the syringe might be broken. The sedative drugs could have expired. The drug might not be working on this particular individual—everyone is different. Or . . .

"In field science," says Pati, "we always make these careful plans. But part of the work we do is figuring out what to do when things go wrong."

7:50 a.m.: Eduardo determines that some drug was delivered—but not enough to knock the tapir out. "It could be dangerous to give more drugs," says Pati. But we can't let him go now, while he's woozy. He could fall into water and drown; his wobbly gait could attract a puma. At least in the trap he's safe. "We'll leave him to recover," Pati adds. "We'll check the rest of the traps and come back and see what to do later."

We drive to the next trap. While Pati walks the short distance to peek in, we dig in to our first food since 4:00 a.m.: a picnic of bananas, toast, and boiled eggs. But before the eggs can be peeled, Pati is back with news.

"We really have to rush! It's a big tapir! This has never happened before—two in one day!"

Pati calls off the attempt to sedate the young tapir.

The radio collar, tools, and spare sedatives are set out on the bandana used to cover the tapir's eyes.

Pati races the car at forty miles per hour—much faster than she would normally drive in the sandy track. A six-banded armadillo scurries by, a scaly-looking fellow who is also unexpectedly hairy (in fact this species is also called the hairy armadillo). A band of coati, long-snouted relatives of raccoons, canter through the grass as if pursued by their tall striped tails. A family of capybaras slide into a *baía* and begin to swim. But we rush on. We need to free the captured tapir as soon as possible—but first we have to check the other traps to make sure others aren't waiting, too. Though it's only 8:00 a.m., it's already 90 degrees, headed to over 100. That can be rough on an animal caught in a trap who is worried about getting out.

Pati's mind is on the two tapirs we already have. She thinks she's seen them before. Back in May, the team captured a young male tapir in the same trap the big tapir is in now. Pati will check the photos she took of him to make sure, but she thinks the youngster in the trap is the same young male, a fellow she called Tonico. And the big tapir in the other trap might be Tonico's mom! On camera-trap photos she's repeatedly seen pictures of a healthy young female with a black scar on her backside, often with a youngster. Pati has been particularly eager to collar her.

"If there's a third tapir, though, I'm going to have a heart attack," says Pati. And a moment later she nearly does. Tracks show that another tapir entered a third trap—but didn't trip the door. Usually we'd be disappointed, but now we're thankful!

By 9:38 a.m. we've checked all the traps, and we're back with the young tapir. In the fierce heat we've sweated off all our sunscreen and insect repellent. But the tapir, of course, doesn't have any of that and would rather hide in the forest to escape the day's heat and the bugs.

"It's too hot," Pati says. "I'm going to release him." But first she takes some quick photos to confirm what she already knows: from the white spots on his lips and ears she can see that this really is Tonico!

While we hide behind trees, Gabriel climbs atop the trap to lift open the door. Tonico trots out calmly—a perfect little gentleman.

10:10 a.m.: At the neighboring trap, the team lays out the equipment. Everyone works quietly, whispering in Portuguese and English. Pati straps a high-def video camera to her blue baseball cap to record the collaring and sampling for later review.

10:35 a.m.: José's dart pistol sounds. Pati reports that the tapir is lying down. "But we have to wait a little before we go in." One thing's for sure, though: this *is* Tonico's mom. Pati recognizes the black scar on her backside from the camera-trap photos.

11:00 a.m.: Usually it takes fifteen minutes for the drug to take effect. We've been waiting twenty-five.

11:05 a.m.: "She's asleep!" Pati announces. She and José climb inside the trap with the four-hundred-pound animal. They cover the tapir's open eyes with the bandana. Top priority is radio collaring the tapir. José and Pati

quickly choose the larger of the two collars they've brought and fit it snugly around the mother's neck. José climbs out, and Eduardo climbs in.

From the gap between boards Dorothée checks the pulse oximeter, a device that passes an infrared light through small blood vessels to check oxygen in the blood. In hospitals, the probe is placed on a person's finger; Dorothée uses the tapir's ear. The reading is healthy: the tapir's blood is full of oxygen (96 percent). Dorothée takes her pulse (64 beats per minute) and checks her breathing (16 breaths per minute). Pati is busy with the tape measure: the female tapir is 211 centimeters (nearly 7 feet) from snout to tail, and, from rear hoof to the top of her back, 110 centimeters (just over three and a half feet) tall. Pati measures her legs, her ears, her head . . .

And then she tells Dorothée with surprising calm, "The tapir is awake." Dorothée instantly fills a syringe with a supplement of one of the sedatives, ketamine, and passes it between the boards to Eduardo. He puts the tapir back to sleep.

Eduardo takes blood from the tapir's front leg, to be examined later in a lab to look for disease. Pati pulls back the tapir's lips to examine the teeth; the wear shows that this mother is fully adult, though still relatively youthful. Everyone helps to pick ticks off the tapir. There are hundreds of them, at least five different kinds. Pati wants to find out about them, too—especially since some of them are on *her* now!

11:30 a.m.: Eduardo quickly implants the microchip behind the tapir's left ear. He sprays the tapir's cuts with purple disinfectant.

11:31 a.m.: Dorothée hands Eduardo the syringe containing the drug to reverse the tranquilizer. The tapir's white-tipped ears twitch. Pati and Eduardo climb quickly over the wall just as the huge animal rises to her feet. She shakes the cloth off her eyes. Grog-

gily, she raises her great snout and flares her nostrils to get her bearings.

11:40 a.m.: The tapir is ready for freedom. José opens the door. The tapir backs out of the trap, stubby tail first—the new radio collar may make her feel as if her head is stuck in something. She spins, turns, and crashes into the bush.

Pati is overjoyed. "She's a beautiful, fat, healthy young female—and we were dying to capture her!" she says. "We were seeing all these pictures of her, and now we have her! This is fantastic!"

Now, what to name her? Pati has already decided. She often names tapirs in honor of students and professionals who volunteer with the project. But Dorothée is difficult to pronounce in Portuguese. So she will name this beautiful young mother after a very special vet and also after the heroine of a series of children's books—one of which even features an adventure with tapirs. For months or years ahead, thanks to her new radio collar, this young female tapir will help us explore the frontiers of knowledge of her kind. What better name for her than Dora the Explorer?

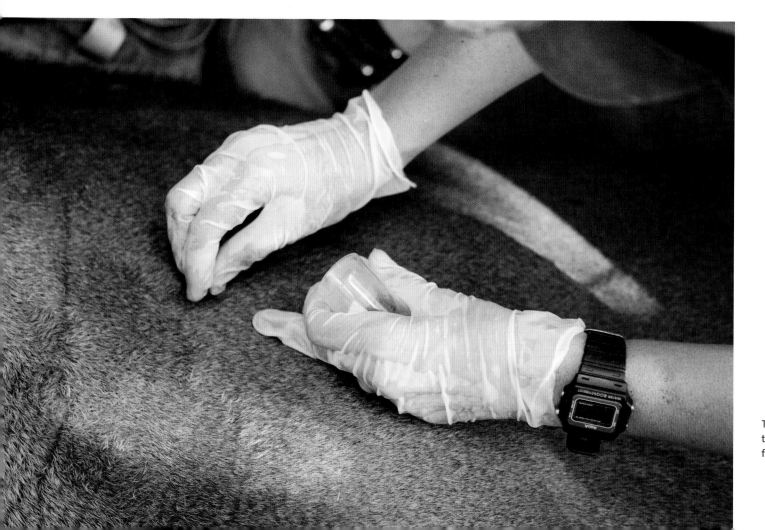

Ticks from the sleeping tapir are stored in vials for later examination.

Tapir Ticks

They're itchy, they're ugly, and they love to suck blood—ticks' only food. But you've got to admire these tough little suckers. They're remarkably successful and found on all sorts of critters all over the world.

Even though they are tiny creatures, ticks seem nearly indestructible. They're almost impossible to squash—because like all insects and spiders (ticks are eight-legged and related to spiders), their skeletons are on the outside. In fact, to grow, they have to shed their skeletons—which is the first thing they do after they finish their blood meal and drop off their host. Most ticks do this three times in their lives.

Ticks are the very soul of patience. Some species can wait more than a year for a meal. They don't really hunt, but they wait in a good place, often in the grass. Most ticks can sense color, movement, and the carbon dioxide from an animal's breath, so they can catch a ride when a good host brushes past.

Sounds like a simple strategy, but it works. There are at least 850 different kinds, and to make things more complicated, each goes through several different life stages: they start as eggs, hatch into tiny larvae (with six legs), then shed their skins to become nymphs (which look like small adult ticks), and finally shed again to become adults, ready (with their next blood meal) to fertilize or lay eggs of their own. Each adult female can lay as many as ten thousand eggs.

Some ticks infest birds (one kind prefers penguins!); some attack reptiles; some infest mainly mammals; and a few like humans. So far, here in the Pantanal, Pati's tick expert, Marcelo Labruna at the University of Sao Paulo, has identified four different species of ticks from the tapirs at Baía das Pedras. But as Pati says, that's *so far*—there could well be more.

Why study tapirs' ticks? An adult female tick (they grow bigger than males) can suck enough blood to increase her weight six-hundred-fold from a single meal. A heavy infestation of ticks can suck so much blood they can give an animal anemia—a deficiency of red blood cells so severe it can leave the animal weak and listless. It happens to horses, it happens to moose . . . and it almost certainly happens to tapirs.

Tapirs probably don't like ticks any more than we do. Ticks cause itching—usually an allergic reaction to their drool—and they're hard to remove. That's for two reasons. Ticks secrete a cementlike substance that literally glues their mouth in place while they're feeding. And the rod-shaped structure with which they pierce the skin of their host is covered by tiny projections, like little fishhooks, which they don't withdraw till they're good and ready—which in many species of ticks takes twenty-four hours or more. So what's a tapir to do? Other researchers have told Pati that tapirs wallow in the mud to try to dislodge the parasites. She hasn't seen this in the Pantanal, but she has seen tapirs get rid of ticks another way: they wait till a bird lands on them and uses his bill to deftly tweeze them off. Everyone (except the tick) wins: the bird eats the tick for a juicy, high-protein snack.

What's most important to Pati is that ticks can transmit sickness from one animal to another. Disease-causing organisms can live in tick drool. One kind of tick she's found on her tapirs, known as the cayenne tick, can carry typhus and horse diseases. (It's the larvae of these ticks that were always on our clothes; luckily, in this area, they don't transmit disease to humans.) Can these ticks bring diseases to tapirs? That's another mystery Pati is hoping to solve.

Peccaries travel in groups that can number more than a hundred. The raised hairs on this animal's back are a warning that it may charge.

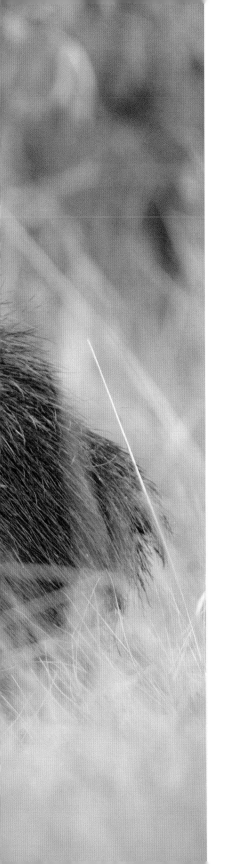

CHAPTER 5

Tapir Troubles

Fresh from the thrill of collaring Dora, we feel lucky. The next morning, Pati asks, "What animal do you want to see today—besides, of course, a tapir?" Nic puts in an order for a giant anteater. Dorothée would love to see the weasel-like tayra. "Today, giant anteater, tomorrow tayra," says Pati. "Positive vibes—it works!"

"All I want to see is a tapir in the sights of my gun," says Gabriel softly. He's determined to dart one. He keeps his door unlatched and his hand on the handle as we drive, dart gun at the ready.

That evening, Nic's wish came true—or a smaller version of it, anyway. Just before dark, right beside our car, we spotted a new animal trundling by. Only about two feet long, with a grasping tail and huge black claws, it sported light yellow fur and black markings that made it look as if it were wearing a sleeveless black vest. It wasn't a giant anteater—but a lesser anteater, also called a tamandua (TUH-man-DOO-uh). Like its much larger relative, it eats ants and termites, up to nine thousand a day, licking them up with a long, sticky tongue. Its strong claws can tear into a termite nest as hard as concrete, and its grasping tail makes the tamandua equally at home in trees and on the ground.

Alas, our good vibes didn't hold for tapirs. We saw none on our morning's drive. We'd had no luck the night before, either. When we checked the traps, the door to one of them was closed—but no one was inside. At another, despite "a tapir highway" of tracks in the sand, no tapir. At a third, footprints showed where a tapir had entered the trap and had even enjoyed a lick at the salt in the trough inside. But the trap didn't spring, and the tapir got away.

A different trap *did* spring. But inside, to everyone's dismay, we found two very angry white-lipped peccaries, piglike animals that travel in families and are smart, swift, and strong enough to kill a jaguar with their saberlike tusks. They clicked their teeth menacingly, a hair-raising sound, like someone cocking a loaded gun.

More frustration followed. One morning, just as the sun was rising, we got a clear view of a big adult tapir. Gabriel and José were ready. Everyone performed perfectly. Careful to make no noise, the men didn't close the car door—and when the vehicle filled with mosquitoes, we didn't even slap. An itchy half-hour later, the men returned to tell us that the tapir, a lovely large female, had veered off to our left, then circled and run into a patch of forest. They could never get closer than seventy yards.

Another day, to our joy, we found a young male tapir in one of our traps—big enough to radio collar! But like Benjamin Martlet and Tonico, despite several shots of tranquilizer, he never showed any signs of sedation. "I've never seen anything like this," said Pati.

This could be a big problem.

To find out what's going wrong, Gabriel and José take turns wrapping tree trunks with cowhide to simulate tapir skin and shooting them with darts filled with water instead of tranquilizer. Then they examine each dart. How far did it go into the leather and bark? Did the shaft break? Did the syringe release the water? The gun and darts seem to be working. Could the drug be the problem? Pati checks to see if it has expired: No, it's fresh.

The next morning, Gabriel reports that he had a nightmare: we saw tapirs, and he darted one—and it turned out that it already had a radio collar.

After the past few days, that's about the only thing that hasn't gone wrong.

Not only are the darts not working; having shot so many tranquilizer darts, now we're running out of sedatives. The drugs are expensive, and to get more demands time we don't have—a twelve-hour roundtrip drive, mostly over dirt roads, to the city of Campo Grande.

Also, the grinding noise in Pati's old Toyota is getting worse. It might be scaring tapirs away. We've borrowed Rita's jeep for the meanwhile—but now, even that vehicle

is complaining. If the jeep gives out, Pati says, we might have to resort to checking traps riding the ranch's horses. That will make long, hot days many hours longer. And in addition to our tick bites, we'll have saddle sores.

Pati is still optimistic. "It's a great place, it's a beautiful place, we've got a great team," she explains, "but this isn't like a laboratory. Things go wrong in the field. We always have to change plans."

She's been through worse before. In field science, some of the most valuable data turns out to be discovering what *doesn't* work.

When she was researching her thesis in the Atlantic Forest, she and her team spent a total of 120 nights without sleep on an observation platform in a tree, above salt bait. Three people on the team came down with skin sores from leishmaniasis, a disease transmitted by biting flies. They were sitting in the bugs and the heat all night without speaking—waiting to see tapirs that never appeared. In all that time, they saw only one. When they tried darting it, the dart fell out, so the animal was never collared. But they made an important discovery: this was not an effective way to catch tapirs. (The most effective method? The box traps we are using now.)

Pati is always working on several fronts, experimenting with different methods and using multiple tools of study. So while the team tries to figure out what's wrong with the darts—and while Pati awaits the mechanic who's coming from Campo Grande to examine her car—we check up on the tapirs we've already collared.

How? Along a particular fence where Pati likes to check the telemetry, she dials up some of her tapir friends: Dora, channel .84; Luis, channel .15; Felippe, channel .08.

"We locate the tapirs by triangulation," Pati explains. Along this fence are fixed "triangulation stations"—reference points from which longitude and latitude are recorded. Dialing up your tapir, you swing your antenna to search for that animal's frequency and find the direction from which the signal comes in strongest. Then, with the same kind of compass you might have used in Scouts, you note the bearing. Dora's signal comes in weakly. The compass needle points to 114 degrees from due north. We tune in Luis. He's at 96 degrees.

This means that if you walked in that general direction long enough and if the animal stayed still, you would eventually run into the tapir. But you don't have to see the tapir to find where it is. To get an animal's location, you need at least two readings. We drive a few thousand yards farther along the fence to the next station, dial up Dora, and listen for her signal again. It's coming in stronger now, strongest at 164 degrees. On a map on her computer back at the ranch Pati will plot two lines representing the two bearings from the two different locations. "Where the lines intersect," she says, "there's the animal!" Luis's bearing is now 164 degrees, too. "They are close!" says Pati. "They could even be together." Maybe on a tapir date?

The telemetry signal also tells whether the animal's head is moving or still. A rapid pulse means an animal is moving. Dora was resting when the first reading was taken, but she was moving during the second. (Maybe she was shaking her head, still unused to the new collar.)

Pati is using two kinds of telemetry collars: Kelly, Dora, Luis Uruguaio, and Felippe Lion have VHF (very high frequency) radio collars; Rita Fleury, Vivek Tudor, and Morena have GPS (global positioning system) collars. The GPS collars are far more expensive (each costs about $3,000, versus about $450 for a VHF collar), but with them, you don't have to physically follow your tapir to find out where the animal went. And you can get lots of data. The GPS collars collect location information by communicating with satellites orbiting the earth, automatically storing these positions in their memory units. The collars are programmed to drop off the tapir's neck when the battery is dead, and they transmit a special signal so you can find them. Then you can download fifteen months' worth of data—provided the collar stays on that long. Sonia Westminster's collar fell off after only fifty-five days. Luckily, Pati found the collar—and discovered that it had already recorded, with dates and times, eight hundred different places Sonia had gone.

Telemetry readings tell important stories. For instance, over time, they can show us a map of an animal's home territory—and whether this changes. This is essential information if you're setting aside land to protect animals; you need to know much land each one needs. And with multiple animals collared, a researcher can learn who hangs around with whom and even how neighbors get along. For instance, when Bandaid was first captured, his tooth wear showed that he was a very old tapir. In captivity, tapirs can live into their thirties. His blood work came back positive for two livestock diseases—leptospirosis, a bacterial disease that can make an afflicted cow abort her calf, and bluetongue, a virus that makes the tongue turn blue and can cause fever. But Bandaid looked fat and healthy. A year of tracking showed that he had a large territory, 311 hectares (768 acres, more than one square mile). When he was recaptured a year later, he still seemed strong and vigorous. In April and May of that year he was found inside his usual territory. But in June no one could find him! A month later he showed up far from his home range. And shortly after that his collar started giving an upsetting, rapid pulse—the signal that he hadn't moved in twenty-four hours. The team tracked the collar to find, sadly, that their old friend had died.

Why did Bandaid abandon his regular territory? Another tapir's telemetry readings suggest one possible answer: the young, healthy Luis Uruguaio moved into Bandaid's area just as Bandaid moved out. Did the younger tapir drive old Bandaid away? Why did Luis want Bandaid's territory anyway? Was it the food, the cover, or the neighbors?

"It's so complicated, I might never figure it all out!" said Pati. But she's determined to try. To do so, she'll need all the clues she can get. And some of the most intriguing clues come from traps that never capture tapirs—except on film.

Burrowing owls perch by the entrance to their burrows or on nearby fence posts, waiting to catch lizards, insects, and small rodents.

Camera traps are powerful tools for studying the lives of secretive animals such as tapirs.

CHAPTER 6

Tapir TV

CLICK-CLICK-CLICK-CLICK-CLICK! On June 1 at 6:11 a.m. the camera's quiet, rapid-fire shutter caught the images of the two lovers together. But this wasn't the work of the paparazzi photographing celebrities for *People* magazine; it was one of Pati's camera traps. When she downloads the images to watch them, she calls it "Tapir TV."

On that morning, Benjamin Martlet and Dora were seen together at a popular tapir meeting area: the Latrine. In fact, in tapir land, the Latrine is a great place for a tapir date. It sounds smelly, but that might be the point. Though tapirs can leave dung or urine anywhere, they often seem to make a special trip to leave it in this particular place. Many animals, from tigers to deer, leave scent messages in their droppings for others of their kind to decode. That's why the Latrine is a perfect spot for one of Pati's camera traps. She's hoping it might reveal the secrets of tapir love life.

CLICK-CLICK-CLICK-CLICK-CLICK! July 12, 6:19 p.m.: Benjamin Martlet is again photographed with Dora at the Latrine. Might this be a lasting relationship? It's not unheard of in tapirs. Surprising studies of the Baird's tapir, the lowland tapir's more northerly cousin, suggest that this species lives in families, both male and female sharing their territories with their current calves as well as older offspring. Pati didn't find this to be true when she studied the lowland tapirs in the Atlantic Forest. But who knows? Things could be different in the Pantanal.

CLICK-CLICK-CLICK-CLICK-CLICK! July 28, 5:31 p.m.: Now Benjamin Martlet is back at the Latrine again. But who's the lady tapir with him this time? It's—Rita Fleury! What's going on?

Turns out that Benjamin Martlet is quite the tapir about town.

"When Benjamin was captured in 2009, remember, he was with *Kelly*," says Pati. Then in August 2010 Benjamin was seen with a female with a baby. But this female didn't have a radio collar. The mom wasn't Rita. "It could be Dora and Tonico," Pati says. "Benjamin could be Tonico's father!"

These are exactly the sorts of relationships Pati hopes her camera traps will reveal. As a scientist, her job is similar to that of a detective solving a mystery. But the stories the camera traps tell sound more like a soap opera.

A picture may be worth a thousand words, but one photo alone can't begin to tell the story. Pati uses cameras that snap five photos,

Benjamin and Dora walk past the camera trap.

Benjamin and Dora return.

Benjamin walks past with Rita.

as fast as two frames per second, one after the other, so that she can see both the front and the back of the tapir. That way she can usually tell who it is, or at least if it's male or female, and whether the tapir is alone or with company. Selecting the right spot and the right angle for each camera is important. The camera projects an infrared beam (like the pulse oximeter's beam, it's outside the spectrum of light that humans or tapirs can see) to a receiver across from it. When an animal crosses the beam, the receiver sends a pulse to the camera, telling it to set off the rapid-fire shutter. It's all recorded on memory cards that can each hold thousands of photos—full color if taken during daylight, black-and-white if at night—which Pati downloads to her computer.

"The camera traps let us into the tapirs' personal lives," Pati explains. Like looking forward to the next episode of a favorite show, she can't wait to tune in and see what's on "Tapir TV."

Some nights are busier than others. One day we checked a camera trap and found it had taken 80 pictures. At another, 225 pictures were taken in a single night. "We have something interesting here!" Pati said as she plucked the disk to take it back to the ranch and reset the camera.

Not all the drama is about tapirs. Any animal who passes by is photographed. Pati gets pictures of ocelots and peccaries, the tall legs of seriemas—and, once, the curious face of a puma who was sniffing the lens.

But over time, the images give intriguing glimpses of the tapirs' secret lives. For instance, even though Pati had tracked old Bandaid with her telemetry and seen him in the flesh a handful of times, she saw him much more often in camera-trap photos.

When the cameras revealed his image on her computer screen, she felt as if she were seeing an old friend. "When he died, I was super sad," she said. "He had become part of my life.

"I want to add more camera traps, to learn what female is with what male, and I want to be able to see when the females have babies with them. It will be really hard to figure this all out," says Pati, "but it's so interesting! The cameras are wonderful in letting me see a lot more of what they do. Now it feels like I'm getting much closer to them."

Who hasn't had that same feeling about an actor, musician, or athlete you've seen on TV but maybe never met?

So when the team finally caught Dora, for Pati it was almost like meeting face to face with a favorite starlet. "We had pictures and pictures of this female tapir with that mark on her butt, and she was here, and she was there," said Pati. "She had a baby. We dreamed of how wonderful it would be to capture her. And so it was really great when we had her in the trap, and looking at her butt—and realizing, it's really *her!*"

Pati's Spreadsheets

What's the most effective way to catch a tapir? What time of day are you most likely to see one? Which habitats do tapirs seem to prefer? Are males easier to dart than females? Are you more likely to see a tapir when the weather is hot and dry, or wet and cool?

These are the sorts of questions Pati is asking all the time. You might think that after a year or two of study Pati and the rest of the team could answer these questions off the top of their heads. But that's wrong. For one thing, people tend to remember last week better than last year. A long drawn-out hunt ending with a dramatic darting is more memorable than a trap capture, when everything goes fast, without a hitch. It's easy to lose track. And it's really important to get the answers right. "We need an idea of what works and what doesn't work," Pati says. "That way, I can look at the data and re-adapt our methods. And later, we can help other scientists when they start their own projects."

That's why Pati records every aspect of all the variables of each sighting and capture and carefully tracks her data on spreadsheets like the ones on the next two pages. It's a method you can adapt to your own study—whether you're watching the squirrels in your yard or the neighbor's cat or an exotic jungle creature.

By carefully recording, organizing, and comparing the data, Pati can answer important questions, such as: How many nights on average can you expect to leave a trap open before it catches a tapir? (The average right now seems to be about five nights.) What method yields more successful dartings—walking or driving? (So far, in the Pantanal, at least, it seems to be driving.)

Scientists have different ways of displaying their data to make it easier to see important patterns. Often, Pati plots her data on a graph. What are the best hours of the day to see a tapir? Pati's graph shows at a glance: between 4:00 and 8:00 p.m. are the most productive hours. But that's also influenced by weather: "We did have quite a few sightings between eight and eleven a.m.," Pati said, "but that was mainly when it was cold."

So a scientist needs to keep track of all sorts of variables. You never know what turns out to be important. How can you make capture less stressful for a tapir? Pati always records the method and time of capture, who were the vets, what was the drug mixture used and in what amounts, whether the drug was delivered by gun, pistol, or by hand, how long and how well the animal slept, what drug was given to reverse the sedation, and how long it took the animal to wake up. Which factors affect whether a tapir can be successfully darted, like Sérgião, or whether he won't go to sleep at all, like Benjamin? Is it the pressure Gabriel uses in his gun, the drug Eduardo uses in the dart, where the tapir is first seen, whether the tapir is male or female, big or small, the weather, the season, the time? The only way to find out is to collect lots of data on everything—and then examine and compare it all.

The first column is the time of day (on a 24-hour clock); the second shows how many tapirs were seen at that time and what's the best time to look for tapirs. The highlighted numbers show the times when the vast majority of sightings happened—as is shown even more clearly in the bar graph to the right.

OPPOSITE: How many traps over how many nights does it take to catch a tapir? You'll also see Pati keeps track of who got caught. Bet you can even read some Portuguese: can you guess what Anta Escapona means?

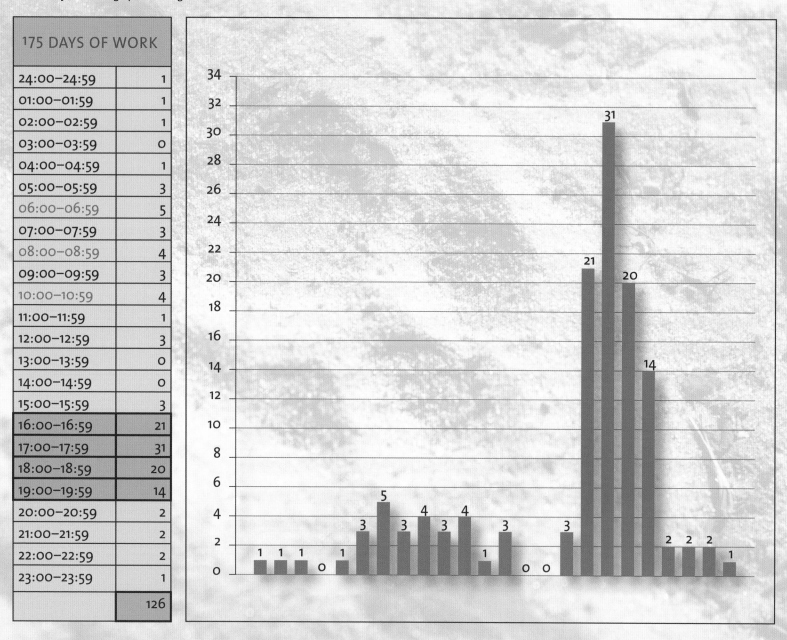

175 DAYS OF WORK	
24:00–24:59	1
01:00–01:59	1
02:00–02:59	1
03:00–03:59	0
04:00–04:59	1
05:00–05:59	3
06:00–06:59	5
07:00–07:59	3
08:00–08:59	4
09:00–09:59	3
10:00–10:59	4
11:00–11:59	1
12:00–12:59	3
13:00–13:59	0
14:00–14:59	0
15:00–15:59	3
16:00–16:59	21
17:00–17:59	31
18:00–18:59	20
19:00–19:59	14
20:00–20:59	2
21:00–21:59	2
22:00–22:59	2
23:00–23:59	1
	126

BOX TRAP CAPTURE SUCCESS RATES

CAPTURE ROUND 07 (NOV 2010)

14 nights	Effort	Trap Nights	Captures	1 tapir/69 trap nights	5 traps open for 14 nights
	5 traps @ 13 nights	65	1	Rita (Rec 1)	
	4 traps @ 01 nights	4			

CAPTURE ROUND 08 (MAY 2011)

14 nights	Effort	Trap Nights	Captures	1 tapir/41 trap nights	10 traps open for 4 nights
	6 traps @ 01 nights	6	3	Tonico, Benjamin (Rec 2), Morena	
	9 traps @ 13 nights	117			

CAPTURE ROUND 09 (AUG 2011)

16 nights	Effort	Trap Nights	Captures	1 tapir/16 trap nights	10 traps open for 2 nights
	10 traps @ 16 nights	160	10	Anta Escapona, Benjamin (Rec 3), Felippe (Rec 1), Tonico (Rec 1), Dora, Sem Nome Soltura, Nic Bishop, Morena (Rec 1), Vivek (Rec 1), Luis (Rec 1)	

CAPTURE ROUND 10 (SEP 2011)

16 nights	Effort	Trap Nights	Captures	1 tapir/38 trap nights	10 traps open for 4 nights
	10 traps @ 15 nights	150	4	Caio, Emilio, Luis (Rec 2), Rita (Rec 2)	
	4 traps @ 01 nights	4			

CAPTURE ROUND 11 (NOV 2011)

16 nights	Effort	Trap Nights	Captures	1 tapir/17 trap nights	10 traps open for 2 nights
	9 traps @ 14 nights	128	8	Dora (Rec 1), Morena (Rec 2), Felippe (Rec 2), Helena, Tonico (Rec 2), Benjamin (Rec 4), Rita (Rec 3), Sachin	
	8 traps @ 01 nights	8			
		950	33	1 tapir/29 trap nights	10 traps open for 3 nights

Pati collects the precious tapir poo.

CHAPTER 7
Tapir Treasures

"Who wants to collect tapir poo?"

Just as we're finishing our picnic breakfast of papaya slices, boiled eggs, and cake, Pati makes an offer we can't resist. To a field biologist, a tapir turd is a treasure. We don't want to ignore any tapir clues, and the droppings Pati has found at the edge of the water here have lots of them. "It's a nice fresh pile!" she calls enticingly. Already she knows something about the animal who left it: "It's from a young tapir," she says. (She's judging from the small size of the squarish briquettes.) Looks like the tapir was here only a few hours ago.

Dorothée holds a plastic container while Pati, wearing latex gloves, stuffs the sample into the vial with a stick. She puts down her stick and, trading her Stone Age tool for a Space Age one, picks up her global positioning system unit. She consults an orbiting satellite to get the precise location of the poop so she can label each sample with the date, time, and place.

"I have three hundred samples in my refrigerator at home," Pati says. The team looks surprised—especially those who've been to her house for dinner. "Not my regular refrigerator," she adds quickly. "It's a special refrigerator just for the poo." She makes it clear that she never gets the two fridges confused!

She's refrigerating all those droppings while she waits to send them to a laboratory in the city. Specialists examine the samples and can tell what plants each tapir has been eating—important data for discovering what tapirs need to survive. Still other tests, on cells shed from the inside of the tapir's intestine, can examine the tapir's DNA, or genetic fingerprint. Pati can learn whether this is a tapir from whom she has already taken skin or hair samples, and if so, which one. She can tell if this tapir is related to any of her other sampled tapirs, to help her fill in the outlines sketched by telemetry readings and pictures taken by the camera traps of who's hanging out with whom. Even back at the makeshift laboratory at the ranch we can learn important information about the young tapir who passed by here, unseen, just hours ago. Looking through a microscope, Dorothée and Eduardo might be able to find out whether the tapir had worms or other parasites living in its gut—and if so, if there were only a few or many, and if the young tapir was sick or well.

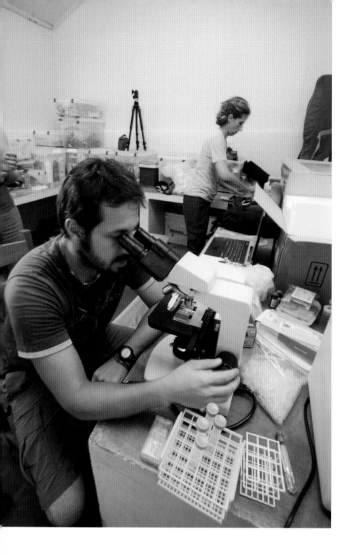

Samples are studied and stored in a small lab the team has set up at the *fazenda*.

"We've got a ton of data here," says Pati, smiling. She reminds us of how much we've accomplished. In just under a week we've collected samples of tapir poop, skin, fur, and blood; located tapirs with sightings, tracks, camera traps, and radio telemetry; radio collared one new tapir and microchipped another. We'll need it all if there's any hope of tracking down the tapirs' secrets: who's who, who's healthy, who's related to whom, who goes where, what's on the menu . . . We're making progress, even if we have hit a hitch with the darting. And that's a situation the team is determined to resolve.

Today we're making several changes. José and Gabriel have decided on a new strategy. In the past they advanced toward the tapir together, about five yards apart, so that José could advise Gabriel with whispers or hand motions. "But there's no way around it," says Gabriel. "It's too bad I won't be able to hear his instructions, but we have to separate. My instinct is to rush forward—like I did that first day. That might have been my best chance at a shot of the whole expedition."

The night before, the rest of the team had stayed up till nearly 1:00 a.m., trying to figure out what to do about the anesthetic. Dorothée suggested that we wait longer between injecting the drug and checking the tapir to see if it's asleep. She, Eduardo, and Pati wondered whether they should change the combination of the sedative drugs—especially given that we're running out of the most expensive one. Luckily for us, right here at the *fazenda* is a young veterinarian whose specialty is animal anesthesia: twenty-four-year-old Caío Filipe da Motta Lima. Caío's been working on a research project on the little-known giant armadillo run by Pati's husband, Arnaud Desbiez, a biologist, who also works here at the ranch. But the giant armadillos seem to be hiding, so Caío agrees to join the tapir team for a few days.

"Anesthesia is tricky," he says, "and it's a big responsibility. There are risks. You are working to conserve the species. The last thing you want is for something to go wrong." He remembers when he was anesthetized himself for an operation two years ago; he woke up confused and terrified. He never wants one of his animals to feel that way.

Consulting with Caío, the veterinarians decide to adjust the mixture of drugs in the sedative. The various drugs all do different things, but they also interact with one another. Butorphanol, ketamine, and medetomidine help the tapir sleep, block pain, and help relax the muscles; atropine protects the heart from the effects of the other drugs. Caío feels that this change will not only help the tapir sleep more deeply and more comfortably; it will also help stretch the expensive butorphanol.

By 9:20 the next morning we've used our telemetry to dial up Luis, and we've located Morena and Dora. We've checked five traps and found them empty. And we've made a new discovery: a new species of tick, a red one, has now joined the legions of tiny ones. Pati picks them off her pants and flicks them out the window as she drives.

By 9:30 a.m. we park by the path to the Acuri trap, which Pati named after the palms nearby. We walk along the large *baía* into the forest (and more ticks) and out again to the wetland, where herons are wading and water hyacinths bloom. By 9:40 we're as close to the trap as Pati wants us to go. José goes ahead to check the trap while we wait in silence.

Egrets are common in the Pantanal.
They wade through water on long
legs, snatching fish and frogs.

"Anta!" José cries. He is excited but cautious. It's a male in the trap, and he is uncollared. But, worries Pati, is it Benjamin? She's not eager to subject him to anesthetic again, even with the new cocktail. But it's not Benjamin! It's a new tapir.

10:15 a.m.: Eduardo loads the dart pistol with the new drug mixture. José goes ahead again, and we wait in silence.

Frogs call. Flies buzz. Is that growling sound coming from a bird, an insect—or one of our stomachs?

10:50 a.m.: The tapir is peacefully asleep. Though he's an adult, he has white spots, like a fawn, on his belly and legs. His many-toed hooves are enormous. The way his snout drapes over his lip gives him a kind, gentle expression. As Pati and Dorothée climb in with him, he starts to snore.

11:26 a.m.: Working rapidly, in under an hour the team has attached the radio collar, taken all the measurements, inserted a microchip, and gathered all the samples. With the new drug mixture, the procedure has gone flawlessly. Through a crack in the boards of the trap, Eduardo hands Dorothée the drug to reverse the sedative. Dorothée and Pati climb out.

11:27 a.m.: The tapir coughs, sending a cloud of dust from the ground into his long, limp nose, and then he sneezes. He stands, tests the air with his trunk, and, noticing the new collar, shakes his head.

At 11:35 a.m. he's steady enough to release. He walks calmly out the open door, turns right, and then, slowly and quietly, vanishes into the forest. It seems he's gone in an instant.

"Muito bem!" cries Pati—that's Portuguese for "very good!" And then in English she declares, "This is fantastic. A brand-new animal! A young adult, very healthy. He didn't even have many ticks!"

What shall we name this handsome new tapir? Nic, who took all the photos in this book, has a suggestion, and Pati agrees: the tapir will be named Nic Bishop!

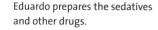

Eduardo prepares the sedatives and other drugs.

Nic Bishop the tapir is ready to join Pati's growing list of study animals.

Giant Armadillo Team

"This is a nice hole!" Arnaud Desbiez, thirty-seven, says admiringly as he peers into a foot-wide burrow on the forest floor at Baía das Pedras.

Pati's green-eyed French husband isn't the only one interested in the hole. Arnaud's camera traps show that foxes, rats, snakes, even tapirs come to investigate these burrows, too. And who wouldn't be intrigued? This hole was made by a prehistoric giant—a giant who's still around, still importantly altering its landscape and intriguing and mystifying scientists. The architect of the hole is one of the least-studied animals on earth: a giant armadillo, a shelled mammal that eats mostly termites yet grows nearly as big as a person, stretching five feet long snout to tail and weighing up to 130 pounds.

Armadillo comes from the Spanish for "little armored one," and most of these tough-shelled mammals are, in fact, quite small. Almost all the twenty-four species of armadillos that grace the earth are less than three feet long (and one, the pink fairy armadillo, measures only six inches).

But, Arnaud says, "once, there were armadillos the size of a VW Beetle." Of the several species of prehistoric giants, he adds, "this is the last one to survive. We're following the last giant of this crazy prehistory. When you're in the presence of this animal, you feel you're traveling time."

No one knows how many giant armadillos are out there, but they seem to be very rare. Arnaud and Pati have asked many people who've lived in the Pantanal all their lives, and almost no one has ever seen one. "It's a treasure for Brazil, for South America—a treasure nobody knows about!" says Arnaud. "It could go extinct without anyone noticing."

Arnaud examines a giant armadillo burrow.

2010-07-30 5:50:04 PM   M 1/3   28°C

HC500 HYPERFIRE   RECONYX

Photographed by one of Arnaud's camera traps, a giant armadillo emerges from its burrow and heads into the night.

He's determined not to let that happen. He and his giant armadillo team—on this expedition, that means Caio and fellow Brazilian Danilo Kluyber, thirty-one—are the first group of scientists ever to attempt a long-term study of this ancient giant. "For me, this was a dream project," Arnaud says. "A species I always wanted to see, if only once."

Luckily for Arnaud and Pati, the same place that's so full of tapirs is also a haven for giant armadillos. Arnaud's thirteen camera traps have revealed that at least six of them live here at Baía das Pedras. That was a shock to Rita, who had lived here all her life without ever seeing one!

She had seen their holes but never knew what they were. Like the tapir, the giant armadillo is an "ecosystem engineer" who modifies the environment. Instead of planting seeds, though, the giant armadillo digs holes—lots of them, some quite enormous. A tunnel may run twelve feet deep, then turn and stretch another dozen feet long.

And lots of other animals use them. Giant anteaters. Tamanduas. Peccaries. Six- and seven-banded armadillos. Rodents take refuge here—and then carnivores such as foxes, tayras, and ocelots come to hunt them. Seriemas poke their long bills inside, looking for reptiles such as snakes. Deep in the cool earth, a giant armadillo burrow provides an air-conditioned refuge in the 100-plus-degree heat.

But after digging these immense burrows, giant armadillos abandon them after only a few nights. Why? That's one of the many mysteries the giant armadillo team hopes to solve—and one of the many reasons the animals are so hard to study.

The best bet is to find and stake out a burrow on the very day it's dug—and that's hard to do on the enormous ranch. So far in the study, it's happened only three times. The first armadillo they caught was named Diego, in honor of a nine-year-old friend. The boy came with his parents and two older sisters to Baía das Pedras from São Paulo city for a vacation, arriving the very first day of the giant armadillo study. Diego wanted to be a biologist and was full of questions for the researchers. "He made us feel like heroes," said Arnaud. When the family left, Arnaud promised to stay in touch. So four weeks later, when the team caught its first giant armadillo, they named him after their young friend. Arnaud phoned Diego's parents, who put Arnaud's voice on speakerphone so the whole family could hear the news. Diego was so happy he cried.

Diego and his parents are still friends with Arnaud and Pati, but no one knows where Diego the armadillo has gone. Attaching telemetry to a giant armadillo isn't easy. They've tried bolting it to the shell; they've tried attaching it to the tail; they've even tried surgically implanting it just under the skin. But since giant armadillos are protected by their shell, they often hide in scratchy scrub, which knocks the transmitters off. So far, Arnaud and the team haven't found a way to keep the devices on for long. Meanwhile, the giants have given the researchers moments they'll remember forever.

A few months earlier Danilo and Caío had caught and released another giant. Five nights later they picked up his signal with their receiver as they were sitting in the back of Arnaud's truck. Danilo recalls, "I heard a noise, turned to my right—and he was ten meters away from us!" They thought he'd smelled them and run away. But no. Danilo was seated in the back of the truck with his legs dangling down. The giant walked up to him, inches from his feet. "I stood up in the truck so my legs wouldn't touch him," he said, "and he stood up and smelled me! It was one of the most amazing moments of my time."

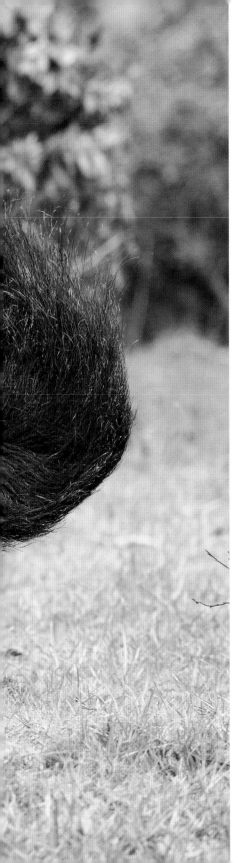

CHAPTER **8**

Tapir Triumph

It's two days later, and a lot has happened. The day after we captured the tapir Nic Bishop, the human Nic Bishop got his other animal wish: a close-up encounter with a giant anteater. Seven feet long, with bold black, gray, and white fur, it's as magnificent as it is unlikely. With a long, thin head and a bushy tail (with which it covers itself when it sleeps), this huge creature has no teeth. It eats nothing but insects, mostly ants and termites. It walks on its front wrists so it won't dull its powerful claws—sharp enough to dig into rock-hard termite nests. We saw it galloping along the side of the track in grassland, its huge tail flying, flaglike, behind.

Later that same morning, we met up with yet another radio-collared tapir at the trap near what we have started to call the Tick Trail. It was Morena—the female radio collared just a few months earlier, named after Eduardo. Pati was glad to see her again, for she'd been worried: tests of her blood drawn at capture showed two biochemical readings Pati thought were "really weird." The vets were per-plexed. One of the readings might have been the result of stress, or might have indicated a chronic disease. Morena had tested posi-tive for swine parvovirus, a disease that can make female pigs infertile. But Morena didn't seem sick at all. Everyone agreed that the way to resolve the mystery was to capture Morena again and draw more blood to see if the values had changed. Here was the chance!

"If I'm finding a disease, I want to know how does it actually affect tapirs," Pati said. But there are other considerations: First, it's hot, over 100 degrees, and we don't know how long Morena has been in this trap. Two: What if the weird blood reading was stress? Should we stress her again? And three: If we're running out of sedative drugs, should we use one of our last doses on an animal who's already been radio collared?

The bottom line for Pati is what's best for Morena. "I really don't want to anesthetize an animal if I don't have to." We set her free. Morena came shooting out of the trap like a speeding bullet.

A giant anteater trots past, holding its wonderfully plumed tail in the air. These unusual animals are surprisingly good swimmers, which is handy in the Pantanal.

sit hunched on hard metal racks in a compartment meant for luggage. It's hot in back, with no windows to roll down. Through a crack in the back door, dust pours into our noses and eyes, getting stuck between our teeth and in Nic's camera equipment. We christen the vehicle "the Dustbin."

Even though Gabriel has one of the "good" seats, next to the door so he can leap out fast, he is unsettled. Though maintaining his humor, he's growing more frustrated by the day. Every day, he's been prepared, alert, and ready—but he has still not darted a single tapir.

Maybe today will be different.

At 5:58 a.m. José cries, "Anta!" It's not just one tapir, but two: a mother and a small baby, perhaps only two or three months old.

Nothing could be more exciting. If Gabriel is able to dart the mother, her baby will stay nearby and we'll get a close-up look at the striped and spotted calf. And if we succeed in collaring the mother, Pati will be able to collect data on the movements of mother and baby at the same time.

We wish we had her energy. The heady mix of thrills and frustration is leaving many of us exhausted. In the early afternoon heat almost everyone but Pati is nodding off to sleep in the car. Waking every day at 4:00 a.m. and eating dinner around 8:00 p.m., no one is sleeping eight hours a night. Everyone has itchy tick and mosquito bites; our field clothes are

getting smelly. Adding to these minor irritations, we've switched to yet another one of the ranch´s vehicles, since Pati's is broken and Rita needs the open jeep for her tourists. This car is quiet, and it's better than riding horses for ten hours straight. But in the space where four of us have to sit, even a suitcase would feel uncomfortable. Nic, Caío, Eduardo, and I

Marsh deer have large, sensitive ears and are always on the alert for jaguars and pumas. They are the largest deer in South America.

Gabriel and José launch out of the Dustbin, running into the predawn dark. Pati leans forward, straining to see through the binoculars. Seeing nothing, she puts her hand to her mouth.

We wait, tense, almost desperate. We want this female so much. Yet we're worried about Gabriel and José. They could be in serious danger. A mother protecting her calf can be fierce. Yet despite our fears, we want to see Gabriel, who works so hard, succeed at what he does best.

As the car fills with mosquitoes, the *Jaó* utters its three-note questioning call. And then the tall orange-legged seriema seems to answer with a series of falling notes.

The sound of disappointment.

The men return. José tells us in Portuguese what happened. He never got closer than forty yards to the mother tapir. Gabriel, according to the new plan, split from his partner and never saw either tapir at all.

The afternoon is windy and cloudy. It's going to rain, but the team departs at 4:30 p.m. in a

rented Mitsubishi truck to try again.

An hour later José spots a tapir. It's standing in the open, quietly drinking from a shallow pool. This tapir is so calm, it even defecates while drinking. Gabriel's dart gun is loaded, and his hand is on the door handle. He sneaks out of the car toward the tapir in a crouching run. José takes another direction.

The tapir doesn't seem to notice. The rental car is quiet; the men are upwind of the tapir, so the brisk breeze carries their scent away. In the squishy soil around the *baía*, the sound of Gabriel's footsteps are cushioned and quiet. No dry, crackling leaves give him away. He approaches to within sixty yards, fifty yards, forty, thirty-five yards of the animal. He can see that the tapir is an adult male. Still, the tapir doesn't seem to hear, smell, or see him. At thirty yards, Gabriel fires squarely at the tapir's rump. It's a perfect shot—until he sees the dart rise with the wind. Gabriel's heart sinks. The wind is carrying the dart away.

But no! The dart hits the tapir just slightly off target, above the hip.

Gabriel drops to his belly. He doesn't want the tapir to know who or what hit him. The tapir turns calmly in the opposite direction and trots across the track on which the Mitsubishi is parked.

In the car, we all hold our breath. On the other side of the track is a larger, deeper *baía*.

Stalking catlike through the swamp grass, Gabriel finally gets close enough for a good shot.

Everyone's worst fear is that the darted tapir will head for the knee-deep water, and there will be overcome by the sedation and drown.

Meanwhile, José, fifty yards from the tapir, sees the dart hit. He's well aware of the water danger and that dark is coming soon. Immediately he starts tuning in his receiver antenna to the frequency of the dart's transmitter. He can't afford to lose track of the tapir. He follows the tapir at fifty yards or so, trying to tune in to the frequency. But the transmitter doesn't work!

Pati gets out of the car and motions to the others to come, bringing all their gear. "*Calma, calma,*" she whispers in Portuguese, urging us all to stay calm as our hearts pound. She heads toward the right of the animal and motions the others to head off to the left. Usually preoccupied with silence, Pati, now twenty yards away from the tapir, runs, yells, and claps her hands sharply to try to herd the tapir away from the deepest water. Groggy and stumbling now, the tapir passes through a seven-inch-deep portion of the *baía* and into an area dotted with small trees. It's nearly dark.

Gabriel has run back to the car through a knee-deep swamp to stow his dart gun in the bed of the truck and grab his headlamp. But now he's lost the tapir. And the rest of the group.

Twelve minutes have passed. The tapir slowly sinks to his knees and lies down.

The team surrounds him. There are no wires or planks separating human and animal, no wall to quickly climb if anyone needs

to escape. "It's dangerous in the forest," Dorothée said later. "You can't anticipate the movement of the animal. It could wake up at any moment." While swarms of mosquitoes bite, Eduardo gives the tapir a second dose of sedative by hand. José has caught up with the group and helps Pati put on the radio collar. Eduardo checks the oximeter to be sure the tapir is doing fine. Dorothée records his pulse. Pati takes the measurements. Dorothée collects the blood samples. Eduardo inserts a microchip. Everyone helps gather ticks.

In Portuguese, José says, "Better take a photo now before—"

At that moment the huge adult male, much larger than the tapir Nic Bishop, stands up.

Eduardo is ready with a shot of muscle relaxant. The stronger dose of sedative used when darting outside a trap can cause muscles to become rigid, he explained, and the

relaxant makes recovery easier, though slower. The tapir sinks to his knees again.

For twenty minutes the team surrounds him, keeping watch. When the tapir rises to his feet, Pati and Eduardo follow him for thirty more minutes as he walks slowly into the field. Only when they are sure he's safe on his own do they return to the car.

When she rejoins the rest of the team, Pati says it's time to name the tapir. "The name of the tapir will be Gabriel, right?"

But Gabriel won't have it. Then what to name this fine, strong male tapir? "Sérgião," he insists. His father's name is Sérgio—but in Portuguese, adding an "ão" makes something bigger. "Let's name him Sérgião—Big Sérgio!"

And just then the rain starts to fall, sounding like applause for a job well done.

The new tapir is a magnificent, healthy individual.

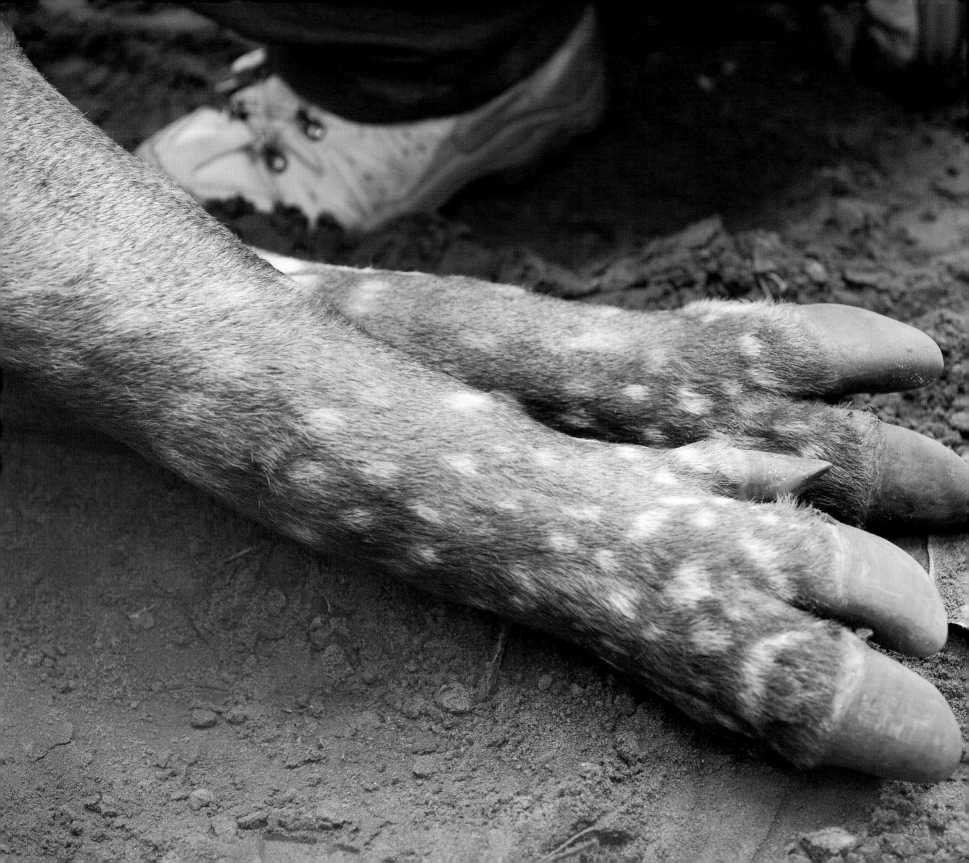

CHAPTER 9
The Tapir Trajectory

For one of our last days on the expedition we've got company. A film crew from Brazil's biggest TV network—Globo Internacional—has come to do a show on Pati's work. "Tapirs have a serious PR problem in Brazil," says Pati. That most people don't know what tapirs are is bad enough. Worse, many people who do know about them think tapirs are stupid. In fact, a slang word in Brazilian Portuguese for someone dumb is *anta*. "But they're not stupid," says Pati. "They're very intelligent. They're almost silent. They're aware of everything around them." They've certainly outwitted our team a number of times. As the long-ago traveler once wrote, the world, perhaps, is "not yet mature enough for their wisdom."

We're eager for people to learn the truth about tapirs. But we're nervous, too. After a rocky start, we've been incredibly lucky. But will our luck hold out? The tapirs, of course, don't know about the film. What if they don't show up for the TV crew?

A year earlier, another crew was waiting at the ranch for the team to return from its evening search. They were thrilled with the news: In the dark, the team had noticed that one of the trapdoors was down. They already had a tapir in a trap! The crew could film its radio collaring and release the following morning.

After an early breakfast, everyone went to the trap. The veterinarians laid out all their medical and scientific equipment. The cameraman, producer, and host filmed it all. Everyone was ready. José went ahead to check on the tapir. But when he came back, Pati said, "It looked like he was about to cry." He pulled Pati aside and whispered, "It's a feral pig!"

Pati laughs as she tells the story. That crew did eventually film a tapir, and maybe this one will, too. She warns the crew of what we already know: you can never predict what will happen with wild animals. That's what makes fieldwork endlessly exciting.

The weather has changed. The cold front that brought rain the night of Sérgião's capture has dipped temperatures so low that we've exchanged our sleeveless shirts for polar fleeces, scarfs, and hats. Pati knew it would be too cold to look for tapirs at 4:00 a.m.; gratefully, we slept in till 6:00. But would the cold weather keep the tapirs from our traps?

Vivek's front legs are elegantly spotted.

Pati photographs Vivek Tudor's distinguishing marks while Dorothée does a health check with her stethoscope.

One, two, three traps are empty. But at 8:43 a.m. Pati returns from the trap where Nic Bishop had been captured just four days before. With a huge, bright smile, she points her thumb up. Another tapir! And this one with no radio collar!

We can't believe our luck. "Since I've been working with tapirs," José tells me through Gabriel, "this is the best campaign I've ever seen. There hasn't been one like this one. Not even projects with other animals are this successful!"

Dorothée is almost breathless: "We are living a great trip, a great moment. This is *wow!*"

Gabriel tells me, "This is almost surreal. So many animals have gone into the traps. And then, when it came time for my shot, the wind almost took my dart—but it went where it needed to go!"

Pati agrees. "This is the single most special expedition in the history of the project. We usually capture or recapture two to three tapirs and are insanely happy when we do. We have never, ever captured or recaptured so many tapirs in the same expedition—this is unheard of."

And there's even more good news: this tapir looks like an old friend—a tapir Pati captured nearly two years earlier but had never seen again.

The sedation goes perfectly, and Pati climbs into the trap with Dorothée. We all creep closer for a look.

Though the tapir is an adult male, he has beautiful light spots on his legs and belly and even on his stubby tail, like a baby would have all over its body. The pattern of the spots confirms what Pati suspected: this is the long-lost Vivek Tudor. Though he was one of the original tapirs collared in September 2009, named after the Westminster Under School houses, Pati and the team were never able to get a single reading from the telemetry. They had never seen him again. Had the collar fallen off? Or just the GPS unit? Or worse, they'd worried, had something bad happened to him? "It's good to get a second sampling, a second capture," says Pati, "but it's *great* to know he's alive!"

Pati and the team won't find out till later, but when she looks over the latest pictures from the camera traps, she will see that Vivek had been checking out this trap for several days. He returned five times before he finally was captured inside. In one picture, taken at 2:30 a.m. three days before, Vivek comes from the direction of the trap, turns, and looks at the camera. He is hyperalert, ears forward, his tapir senses fully engaged. He pauses mid-step, thoughtfully sampling the night's scents and sounds, weighing their meanings in a way humans will never know. The photo captures him with one hoof raised, making his four-hundred-pound bulk look as graceful as a ballerina.

Now, as he lies here before us asleep, Vivek's calflike spots make him seem younger and more vulnerable. The way his trunk hangs over his mouth almost makes him look as if he is smiling, dreaming a happy tapir dream.

We can't know what or if Vivek is dreaming, but Pati often speaks about her own dreams: "My dream," she says, "is to see the lowland tapir studied in all the habitats where it lives." And there's more: "I want people to hear about tapirs on a regular basis. I want them to know why researchers are dedicating their lives to conserving tapirs. My dream is that people everywhere care about tapirs. Otherwise, how will we save our biodiversity?"

After all, tapirs, she reminds us, are the gardeners in the forests, dispersing seeds and regenerating trees. If it weren't for tapirs, many of the other animals that feed on the

Vivek Tudor.

fruits and leaves of these trees might disappear—and so would such carnivores as jaguars and pumas, who eat these plant eaters to survive. Conservationists recognize tapirs as an "umbrella species"—animals who need large amounts of land and often different habitat types. If tapirs are protected, that "umbrella" of protection will safeguard many other species as well.

Some might call Pati's wish an impossible dream. But looking at Vivek, asleep peacefully before us, it's impossible *not* to want to protect these beautiful, innocent, ancient animals—for the day, perhaps coming soon, when our world is mature enough to appreciate their wisdom.

Vivek wakes up, ready to go.

Epilogue

Nic and I had to leave Baía das Pedras a few days before the rest of the team. By the time we reached the States, great news was waiting for us: Just before packing up, the team had caught another tapir, whom Gabriel had successfully darted just as he did Sérgião. Having already honored the photographer of this book, the team named the active mother tapir for the author: Sy Montgomery.

Sy the tapir enjoys a swim.

SELECTED BIBLIOGRAPHY

Durrell, Gerald. *The Whispering Land*. New York: Viking, 1961.

Lowen, James. *Pantanal Wildlife: A Visitor's Guide to Brazil's Great Wetland*. Guilford, Conn.: Globe Pequot Press, 2010.

Medici, E. P. *Assessing the Viability of Lowland Tapir Populations in a Fragmented Landscape*. Canterbury, U.K.: University of Kent (Ph.D. thesis), 2010.

Pearson, David L., and Les Beletsky. *Brazil: Amazon and Pantanal*. Boston: Interlink Publishing Group, 2005.

TO LEARN MORE . . .

Pati Medici´s website: www.tapirconservation.org.br.

Pati Medici is the chair of IUCN/SSC Tapir Specialist Group (TSG), more than 150 tapir conservationists from 27 countries working to study and protect all four species of this wonderful animal. Visit their website: www.tapirs.org.

Thinking of a trip to the Pantanal? You can stay at the ranch where we worked, where kids are particularly welcome. Check it out: www.baiadaspedras.com.br.

How little do most people know about tapirs? Find out from the short video entry on tapirs for the Wildlands Contest for Emerging Wildlife Conservation Leaders. See it here: www.youtube.com/watch?v=tLi9GrsP7TM.

To convince his classmates to donate money from their fundraiser to Pati's tapir project, Benjamin Brind showed a short video on her work after she had won the prestigious Whitley Award honoring her as an outstanding conservation leader. Go to www.whitleyaward.org.

Pati's team shares videos of many of the tapir captures described in this book. See them on Pati's YouTube channel (www.youtube.com/patriciamedici).

ACKNOWLEDGMENTS

We want to thank all the wonderful people who helped us bring you the words and pictures in this book. Of course, huge thanks go to the scientists, volunteers, and researchers you have met in these pages: Pati, Arnaud, José, Dorothée, Gabriel, Eduardo, and Caío. We're grateful for the warm welcome we received at Baía das Pedras from owners Rita and Carlos, their family, and staff. We also want to thank some folks behind the scenes: our fabulous editor, Kate O'Sullivan; Dr. Marcelo B. Labruna, who generously shared fascinating information about the ticks Pati sends him for identification; Robert and Judith Oksner; Jody Simpson; Sy's husband, Howard Mansfield; and Nic's wife, Vivien Pybus.

A special thank-you to a scientist who was not on this trip except in spirit. Dr. Lisa Dabek, the scientist featured in our earlier book *Quest for the Tree Kangaroo*, suggested Pati's project as the subject of another book for the Scientists in the Field series and generously introduced me to Pati when she and I were both in Seattle for a zoo conservation conference. Boy, are we glad she did!

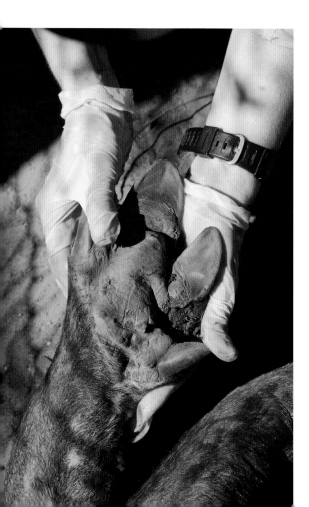

Coatis often feed in groups, chattering with grunts and chirps while holding their bushy tails in the air.

INDEX

Page numbers in **bold** refer to illustrations.